THE SPIRIT
OF
SUCCESS

PRESENTED BY

ADAM MARKEL
Peak Potentials

BILL WALSH
"America's Business Expert"

Presented by: Adam Markel and Bill Walsh

Producer: Ruby Yeh

Editorial Director: AJ Harper

Print Management: Book Lab

Book Design & Typesetting: Chinook Design, Inc.

ISBN-13: 978-0-9891792-3-2

Printed in the United States of America

Contents

A Welcome from Adam Markel   1

A Welcome from Bill Walsh   7

Darin Bullivant
Dream Extreme   13

Fabian Tan
For a Living City   21

Kathryn Cooper
Nowhere to Go but Up!   27

Peter Thompson Moles
Resolution for Reinvention   35

Rhonda Spinks
Pass the Torch   43

Walter Anderson
One Step at a Time   49

Denice Young
Passion Igniting   57

Christine Sherbert
Take Your Time Back   63

Paula Oleska
The Power of Passion   69

CONTENTS

Danielle Nistor
DIVINE CONTRACT   75

Connie K
HEALING HEARTS AND CHANGING HABITS   81

Juliette M. Willoughby, Esq.
BATTLING TOWARD BALANCE   89

Teriann Matheson
EYES WIDE OPEN   95

Dr. Sarah Arnold
HIDDEN IN PLAIN SIGHT   101

Claude Vigneault
ARE YOU OUT OF BALANCE?   107

Tomoko Omori
"IMPOSSIBLE" IS JUST AN OPINION   113

Carey Buck
STOP ASKING PERMISSION   119

Mara Hoover
ON YOUR TERMS   125

Pam Macdonald
NO REGRETS   131

John Long
CAN'T IS A COWARD'S WORD   139

Sally F. Larson
LIFE CAN CHANGE IN A MOMENT   145

Nicole Mason, Esq.
FINDING TRUE NORTH   151

CONTENTS

Irene Aldrich
REVITALIZING JOURNEY 159

Dagmar Schult
BEYOND LIMITS 165

Lane L. Cobb
LET'S DANCE 171

Carol Smith
SUCCEEDING IN FORGIVENESS 179

Natasha Cooke
THE REMARKABLE ENERGY OF INTENTION 185

Nellie Williams
CHASING SHINY OBJECTS 191

Latonya Collins
STEP OUT OF THE BOX 197

Lauren Ellerbeck
ARE YOU LISTENING? 203

Cheryl Desaritz
WALK AWAY 209

Christene Cronin
LOVING THE PROCESS OF SUCCESS 215

Steven H. Poulos, DDS
JUST KEEP DOING 221

Dr. Eric Wong
SMALL STEPS TO BIG CHANGES 227

A Welcome from Adam Markel
Peak Potentials Training

I was forty years old when I found myself in the emergency room, my wife holding my hand, convinced I was having a heart attack. I was a giant ball of sweat, my fingers tingled and my pulse raced. As I looked down at the electrodes attached to my chest, I thought, *I'm dying. I'm never going to get to see my kids again.*

As we waited for the doctor to give us what I was sure would be bad news, I worried myself into a state. Like a fast-moving slide show, my mind raced, not with pictures of the life I had lived, but with the life I had *yet* to experience. *I am going to leave this earth without accomplishing what I'm here to do. I'm not the person I wanted to become.*

If my friends and colleagues had heard my thoughts that day they probably would have been shocked. After all, I'd accomplished quite a lot—almost everything I set my mind to, in fact. I was blessed with a successful seventeen-year marriage to the love of my life. We had four healthy, fantastic kids. And, despite the fact that I grew up in a home where financial success was not modeled, I had acquired it—first as an attorney, and later as a real estate investor and entrepreneur.

By all accounts, including my own, I was living a successful life. But something was missing. I had sensed that before. In my mid-thirties, I started to believe my life was not my own; I started to question: *Is this all there is.* At the time, I was working seventy to eighty hours a week in my law firm (occasionally even sleeping in the office) and, though I was proud of and appreciated my success, something about my life seemed wrong. I couldn't quite identify it, or articulate it, but I could feel it in my body. Suddenly, I started losing my hair and experienced other physical changes precipitated by the imbalance—the *feeling* that I was missing an important piece of my life.

Though I was earning very good money, I was unhappy with the grind of working, working, always working. It seemed as though my soul was shriveling up on the inside, as though some part of me, some spark, some purpose, was dying on the vine.

This went on for quite a while. Like everyone, I had emotional peaks and valleys, but my valleys left me despondent and confused. I would wake up in the morning with a sense of dread about the day.

Whatever I thought my life might be like when I was a kid (lying in bed on Saturday mornings dreaming of the future), it wasn't turning out that way. Worse, I didn't feel any control over the situation, any ability to move myself onto a different path.

I was living a successful life. But something was missing.

So there I was, horizontal on a hospital bed in the emergency room, convinced I was about to die and sure that I had not become the person I was meant to be. When the doctor came into the room, I expected to hear the worst. Instead he said, "You didn't have a heart attack, you had a panic attack. You're dealing with too much stress, and you should lay off the coffee."

As I sat there listening to the doctor's words, looking at my lovely wife crying tears of relief, it was as if a thousand pounds had been lifted from my shoulders. Leaving the hospital that day, I knew that I had been given a reprieve. I realized I had been given a second chance. I remember looking up to the sky and saying out loud, "Thank you."

Now, that wasn't the only second chance I've been given in my life, but before then I had never spontaneously said "thank you" to God. I believed in God, but I wasn't a fan of organized religion. So in the past, when I got a mulligan, when something went wrong or I was worried that something *would* go wrong and everything turned out okay, I would just take a deep breath and go back to business as usual.

Not this time! This time, my second chance cracked my heart open and compelled me to give thanks. I *woke up* that day. And I wanted more—more connection, more grace, more opportunities

---

My new thoughts started to produce new actions.

---

to express my gratitude. I had received another message; the panic attack was a knock on my door and I fully intended to answer it.

Luckily for me (and you), the Universe is always perfect. When we're tuned in (present, in other words), we receive signals and signs about how to redirect our lives—an idea whispered to us in our dreams, a vision formed in conversation with a friend, a pull toward something when we least expect it. The mystery of our lives is slowly but surely revealed to us when our minds are still and we are open to receive these messages.

Eventually, I responded to those messages; initially, by reading books. It began with Dr. M. Scott Peck's *The Road Less Traveled* and morphed from there into *Awaken the Giant Within* by Tony Robbins, books on spirituality by Emmet Fox and, based on a recommendation from a good friend, *Secrets of the Millionaire Mind* by T. Harv Eker. The personal development books I read opened more than just my neural pathways. Suddenly, my mind was thinking differently and my new thoughts started to produce new actions. Until then, I had not explored or practiced any personal or spiritual development. It was a brand new world, one that dramatically changed the quality of my life and the landscape of my dreams.

In a few short years, my change in mindset yielded me tremendous joy and even more wealth and success. The child of two proud, hardworking parents, I had became a multimillionaire and, through a process of setting new goals for myself, went from attending personal development seminars in my spare time to becoming Lead Trainer and CEO of one of the world's largest personal development training companies, Peak Potentials.

> ***Open your eyes and feel connected
> to your own highest self.***

I learned what was missing: spirit. In my work with Peak Potentials, I developed a recipe for success that involved three key ingredients, which I will share with you in a moment. What I realized that day in the hospital was that my life had lacked inspiration and the heart-based motivation that comes from being of service to worthy pursuits. I discovered that I am, as we all are, a spiritual being having a human experience and not the other way around.

Without spirit—whatever that means to you, whether the God of your religion or a force in the Universe or something else entirely—we will always search for answers. No matter how we define success, spirit is an essential component for not only attaining that success, but also *appreciating it*, enjoying it, loving it.

In my new book, due out next year through Simon & Schuster, I reveal—for the first time—my tools for personal and professional *Reinvention*, which include, in part, my recipe for success:

1. *A commitment to personal growth.* Tony Robbins uses the term "constant and never-ending improvement" and I adopted that term, but added a word: To be truly successful in life and reach your own peak potential, you must be committed to constant and never-ending self-improvement. When you make a formal

commitment such as this and recommit to it every day, change happens. It's inevitable.

2. *Tenacity.* This key ingredient is missing for a lot of people. We must persist and persevere in pursuit of what we want. Sometimes we take no for an answer because we're not clear about what we want, so complete *clarity* is essential for harnessing tenacity. Remember, if your habit over time is that you don't show up with tenacity, your life will be a reflection of that mediocre level of energy.

3. *Rituals.* Divinity lives in each of us. If we start each day with the ritual of tapping into, using and touching the divinity within in order to connect with other divine beings, we begin each day in the spirit of success. This was the missing ingredient I had been searching for in my thirties. Begin each day in gratitude, prayer and forgiveness.

It's not like I'm a genius. These are universal laws; I didn't make any of this up. Universal law applies equally to all. It does not make judgments. If you have clarity about what you want, you move tenaciously to get it and you live in a state of appreciation and gratitude each day. You'll get what you want and, oh, so much more. This is the powerful, transformational energy of creation. Use it wisely.

Today, rather than start each day with dread, or with some mysterious sense of feeling unfulfilled, I wake up and say, "I love my life."

As you'll learn from the inspirational true stories in this book, it is not one thing that defines success; it is the *spirit*, the intangible, that makes a person feel successful, happy and fulfilled. Spirit is with you always to produce authentic success and enables you to experience it fully.

C.S. Lewis said, "You are never too old to set another goal or dream a new dream." That's a great quote to describe the kind of person that is part of Bill Walsh's and my family and our co-authors in this book. Let their stories inspire you to heed the messages in your own life that direct you to the right path. Let their stories empower you to follow your heart; not just in thought, but also in deed. Let their stories empower you to continually move forward, even if you don't know how to do something, even if your world is full of naysayers, even if you tried once before and failed.

Ground yourself in the blessing that is your life. Open your eyes and feel connected to your own highest self. It is through *spirit* that true success is achieved and what is missing is found.

Adam Markel was named CEO of Peak Potentials in November 2011. He is a master trainer in the areas of personal and business development, a keynote speaker, bestselling author, real estate developer, entrepreneur and attorney. Having run his own private law practice for more than seventeen years, Adam went on to focus his attention on creating a successful commercial real estate investment firm, title insurance company and social media start-up. Returning to his roots as a teacher, Adam has trained thousands and thousands of students in Singapore, Malaysia, Vietnam, Australia, Europe, Canada and the United States.

One of the most charismatic speakers you will ever see, Adam trains from his heart, believing that honesty and support bring out the best in people. He treasures the opportunity to be a role model to people who hope to have amazing relationships, successful businesses and time-freedom to pursue their lives' missions. He enjoys networking with other successful entrepreneurs and strives to reach out to those who are still struggling. Adam speaks his truth with compassion and finds strength in living authentically and passionately. One of his greatest joys has been raising four amazing children with his wife Randi and empowering them with these same traits. Connect with Adam at www.AdamMarkel.com.

A Welcome from Bill Walsh
"America's Business Expert"

Begin within—from within you can win. It's a simple phrase, yet absolutely critical if you are to achieve your highest vision.

After helping more than a hundred thousand entrepreneurs all over the world launch and build their businesses, I view motivation differently than I did when I first started in this industry. I've realized that, by itself, motivation is empty. If you're feeling unmotivated, it's not because you lack discipline or aren't worthy of your dream; it's a sign that you need to go within and reconnect with your core passion, the dream that will *inspire* you to take action.

When you have a big and bold vision for your business, your life, your community, the planet, that vision will pull you where you need to go. You will have no need for tricks or tips to "stay motivated." When you go within, you win, because you begin with your intuition, that initial spark that guides you and does not judge your "crazy ideas," that spark that inspires you to take the first step and propels you forward until you realize your big vision.

Success is a process, not an event. Some people look at my own success—as one of the leading entrepreneurs in the success education field and founder of one of the biggest seminar companies in the world—and imagine I skyrocketed to these heights in a very short period of time. Like most "overnight" success stories, mine was years in the making. Raised on the South Side of Chicago in a middle class family, I worked my way through the process of success. And I did succeed. But it wasn't until I took time to go within that I was able break through barriers and achieve the level of success I had been working toward for fifteen years.

For years I worked diligently to connect with certain leaders and groups in my industry, but my efforts just didn't work. The definition of insanity is doing the same thing over and over again while expecting different results, so I knew that, if things were going to change, I would have to change. If things were going to get better, I would have to get better.

Success starts with a better you and, for me, that meant shifting my thought process from, "Hey, I'm all that and here's what I got and what I do" to, "Wow, I love what you're doing; let me come up with some ways to help you achieve even more success." I started to realize that to make doors open quickly I had to be perceived, not for great things I'd done in the past, but as *someone who serves first* and expects nothing in return.

This philosophy doesn't come from me. The Bible tells us that to become wealthy we must serve others. Zig Ziglar built on that and said, "You can get everything in life you want, if you will just help

---

Success is a process, not an event.

---

enough other people get what they want." It's not anything new. President John F. Kennedy said it in his own way, too: "My fellow Americans, ask not what your country can do for you, ask what you can do for your country."

Inspired, I focused on how I could serve on the highest level and provide enormous value for whomever I was helping. Once I began to do this, doors that had been closed to me opened wide and with ease. Big companies and some of the world's top thought leaders, people I didn't know well or at all, became my customers and some became my sponsors and marketing partners—people like John Gray, Brian Tracy, Les Brown and Mark Victor Hansen;

companies like Peak Potentials, Success Resources, CEO Space, Infusionsoft and American Express.

As I began to enter into conversations with the top producers in their industries, I realized they really tuned in when I offered to serve them first. Then, when I did help them and got results, guess whom they told? They told everybody. My old attitude of "I'm all this and that" got me a row of closed doors. Why? Because billionaires don't care what you've done, they care that you pay attention and add value to their lives—first. And if you can do that, the people you want to build relationships with *will* pay attention to who you are and what you've done. More important, they will tell people about it.

**I realized they really tuned in when
I offered to serve them first.**

When, in an effort to change my circumstances and better myself, I went within for answers and conceived a bigger vision that inspired me to act, everything changed. Before, my life was about goals and making money, but then I realized that I could do so much more if I came from a place of super-high service.

My inspiration motivated me to turn that message into something that would really work in the business world. Since then, one of my key messages to entrepreneurs is to focus, not on what they can get, but what they can give.

Focus on truly making a difference while you're here on this planet. Then you go from being successful to being significant to the people around you. If you go into business with the idea of service, you're coming from a place that creates value. What I teach is value creators rule—and they make all the money. If you chase money, you'll stay broke. If you chase being number one in your space and adding tons of value, you'll become super wealthy.

The beauty of this is that, when you serve lots of people on a super-high level, you come back to inspiration again. You are *inspired* to act; motivation is not required.

I'll never forget the first time we hosted a Challenge Night as part of our Rainmaker Business program. We asked entrepreneurs to stand up and share stories about the biggest challenges they faced and how they broke through to achieve remarkable success. The idea was that we would give some of our participants a chance to speak from the stage, to be appreciated for the experts they inarguably were, to shine. As it turned out, those who benefited the most were the other entrepreneurs in the audience.

That night I witnessed the transformative power of an inspirational story. One by one, each story touched everyone in the audience. The stories they heard inspired those listening to go

Focus on truly making a difference
while you're here on this planet.

within, to reignite that intuitive spark that, for whatever reason, they had forgotten. What happened after that first night was incredible—so many people went on to claim their own success stories, too many to count.

To offer you an opportunity to be inspired, to reconnect with your own highest vision—that is the reason I wanted to produce this book. Through the stories of ordinary people yielding extraordinary results, we see ourselves having the same success— or different, better, more, bigger, bolder, deeper, higher. Many times hearing someone else's success story triggers our own ability to go within and to remember that we already have all of the gifts we need to realize our highest visions in business and in life.

You are connected to a very powerful source, every day. The question is: Are you going to tap into it and use it or watch other people tap into it and use it? That powerful source is intuition— your gut feeling that tells you the right or wrong thing to do in every situation. And the reason the ninety-eight percent stay the ninety-eight percent is that they don't trust their intuition. Instead, they ignore their intuition, disregard their inspiration and pay attention to the naysayers, the self-doubt and the fear.

My hope is that this book will help you go within and tap into *your* intuition. If this book gives you one more week, or month, or year of hope and inspiration, then we have made a significant difference; then we have succeeded.

It's okay if you don't have all of the answers. Remember, as I wrote earlier, success is a process, not an event. The most successful people in the world paid the full price and paid in advance. Learn what you can from the authors in this book. Use their winning principles and take massive action toward your highest vision. With every page you turn, with every story you read, step further into your amazing self!

Bill Walsh is the CEO and founder of the business coaching/venture capital firm Powerteam International. Bill hosts and speaks at events all over the world. His passion is to empower entrepreneurs and business owners to create massive success. He loves to help people to understand specifically what it takes to build successful companies. He is an accomplished author, speaker, radio personality and movie celebrity. Building on a successful background in finance and marketing, Bill has spent two decades working with firms from start-ups to major global brands to increase sales, productivity and overall success. He is an innovator with a remarkable ability to determine and dictate success strategy to seize global market opportunities.

The Rainmaker Summit and WIN University® programs offered through Powerteam are designed to assist entrepreneurs in creating the focus, plans and partnerships required to build multi-million dollar companies. Through the William Walsh Foundation, Bill provides kids between the ages of twelve and eighteen with the opportunity to be granted free tuition to attend one of the Rainmaker Summits. Through a partnership with Big Brothers Big Sisters, the William Walsh Foundation plans to help more than five thousand students attend the Summit in 2014 alone. Connect with Bill Walsh at www.BillWalsh360.com.

Darin Bullivant

DREAM EXTREME

It was well past 8:30 p.m. when I started to worry about our teammate, Anthony. Racing the second leg of the Baja 1000, he had been riding for an entire day in grueling conditions on Mexico's Baja California Peninsula. Along with Chris and Andre, we were Team D.I.R.T. (Dream It Race Team), four motorcross racers who had trained for months in the hopes that we would finish what is widely known as the toughest race on the planet—and I was set to race the next leg.

Waiting with our support team, Pascal, Alan and Ricardo, I tried to keep my spirits up talking to the Mexicans who were hanging out nearby. When Anthony finally rolled in at 2:00 a.m,, we immediately knew what had taken him so long: his headlight was blinking like a strobe light.

When we expressed our relief at seeing him he said, "I think I'm going to vomit!"

He had been riding this way for eleven hours through the pitch black night and had crashed more times than he could remember. Anthony was covered in dirt and silt, his face, barely recognizable, his eyes filled with grit and dust. Despite all that, he had a giant grin on his face.

All hell broke loose in our pit. The Mexicans swarmed us to watch the happenings as if we were some kind of professional Indy car team. After we tended to Anthony the team readied my CRF 450 X; I pitched in until all was ready. And then there was nothing left to do but smile and give Anthony, Alan, Pascal and Ricardo a huge thank you hug.

"Radio Andre and tell him I'll see him in nine hours!" I said, as I burned a big donut in the sand to impress the Mexicans and rode off down the dirt road to the highway.

My journey to the Baja 1000 began years earlier, when I decided to quit my teaching job to become a stay-at-home dad. It was a dramatic shift for me. My days were filled with house renovations and looking after my girls, leaving space for my mind to run with jealous thoughts about my wife Kelly's past partners. I started to look at her dating history, going so far as to read her old journals, which took me to a really dark, sick place.

At the park with my daughters, I couldn't enjoy my time with them because my heart and mind raced with thoughts of infidelity, as if it were actually happening. When I shared my fears with friends they looked at me as if I was crazy. But for me, it was super real.

It all came crashing down when I realized that I could lose my family. My body was tired and broken from years of reckless behavior, my mind was depressed and my marriage was in trouble. I was messing up. I decided to see a psychiatrist, but I was scared because I didn't want to take drugs.

When I explained my situation to my sister, she said, "Before you go on any drugs or anything, sign up for the Landmark Forum. It's a weekend workshop about understanding your mind and it will make a difference in your life."

I was desperate for a solution so, without hesitation, I said, "Yup, I'm taking it."

By the end of that weekend, I was free. It was so hard, that weekend, to face the truth of my programming. I cried all day Saturday and then Sunday, after having read the concepts ten thousand times over the years, I finally got it: The reality I had created in my head had nothing to do with the real world and I was living the baggage from my childhood and past over and over again.

When I broke free of this pattern of thinking and took responsibility for my feelings and, ultimately, my life, a new joy in living began. I was redefined and reinvented. I decided to get off my butt and stop blaming the world for how my life sucked. My new self knew that I could do anything I wanted to do, so I started to play with my dreams instead of focusing on wanting to change the past. From that moment on, I became the creator of my life, rather than the victim of circumstances.

First and foremost, I went to work on how I was viewing my loving wife and we got our marriage back on track. The concepts branched out to my friends and family as well and many old wounds were healed in that week.

I realized that I could lose my family.

Next, I decided to follow through on my desire to write a book and, with my daughters, created *The Things in Me* and *The Monster in Me*, starter books for children to begin to understand how to become responsible for their own lives.

Growing up, I was a pretty good athlete, but I never went anywhere with it because I never believed I could. Through the conversations with my daughters, helping them to understand the tenets I had learned through Landmark and later at Peak Potentials Training, I came to realize that: "Hey, you're amazing, but you just don't believe it. All you need to do is flip your inner switch and realize that you're the creator and then just go out and get your dreams."

Inspired by my friend Jan Bieber, who had lost two hundred pounds and in the process became an extrreme endurance athlete, I started training for my first marathon. I had torn the acl and meniscus in both knees, broken and separated both shoulders and ruptured both Achilles tendons. An interior voice shouted a long list of excuses for not running, but I didn't listen to that voice. I had learned that that voice was what had prevented me from living a life I loved and doing things I had dreamed about. People say, "I can't run a marathon because I have bad knees." I am living, running proof, that they are wrong.

I set out to transform my body. I tenaciously studied diet and signed up with Mission Fitness to get my body turned around. Every morning, I got up at five to run with Jan and Rick, a holistic nutritionist and elite iron man athlete. We ran rain or shine and sometimes in minus-forty degree temperatures and two feet of snow. I learned about integrity on a whole new level. Then I thought, *I can go bigger than this. I want to make a bigger impact.* I wanted to do something nobody had accomplished, an extreme dream. When delivering forty donated bicycles to orphaned children in

I became the creator of my life.

Baja, Mexico, I fell in love with the area and decided to try to race the Baja 1000—the toughest race in the world.

Before taking responsibility for creating my own life, I never would have considered entering that race. I would have decided I wasn't good enough and that it wasn't even possible to finish—the race was in Mexico; the logistics would be nuts; people had *died* trying to finish that race. It was so over the top for me that I said, "That's it. That's the one."

Recognizing my past limiting belief patterns coupled with my habit of pushing my body in unhealthy ways, I decided I needed an integrity or accountability structure to help me. I chose to compete in a mountain bike race as well as run a marathon before the Baja 1000. That would get my body into the kind of shape needed for the 1000. I had never mountain-biked before, so, naturally, I found the hardest mountain bike series in the world, the TransRockies Challenge and signed up with a knowledgable, fun-loving downhill mountain biker as a partner, aptly named Dave Hart. I also signed up to run the Victoria Marathon with another inspired runner, Jenee Mealey, who would run well below her capabilities to be my pace coach. I hoped that by surrounding myself with greatness, I would increase my chances of success. I called it an Extreme Triathlon and dedicated it to the Children's Wish Foundation. I ended up raising more than twenty-two thousand dollars for the organization and, coincidently, sent an old friend and his family on the trip of a lifetime to Atlantis in the Bahamas. Their daughter, Mya, had a long list of troubles and had spent most of her life in the children's hospital where Kelly works as a nurse practitioner.

My new mindset was put to the test racing in the TransRockies. The race is a punishing grind in the best of conditions, but on our

You're making history every day.

first day my racing partner and I dealt with pouring rain, mud and nastiness for thirty kilometers—straight up and straight down. That first day crushed me; I was devastated mentally and wrecked physically. I couldn't sleep. I lay there, heart pounding, thinking, *There is no way I'm going to survive this.*

In the morning, I got up and washed off the bikes. In the light of day, I was able to flip the switch. I noticed that my suffering was related to my attachment to finishing and having that as my success. I figured once I finished the race I could talk to people and they would listen to me.

I was reliving old patterns of unworthiness again. *I'm not going to listen to those defeatist voices. I'm going to make this the best experience.* That shift in mindset changed, not only the outcome of the race, but also our enjoyment of it. Not only did we finish, we finished with a grace and style that was unprecedented. No matter what challenges we came up against, we were able to solve them and continue racing and we did it with grins and laughter, while others were grumbling and complaining about the weather. We got stronger each day while others were slowly defeated by their thoughts. It was no accident that Dave Hart was my partner that year. We were aligned in thought as well as body and I am honored to know him. Thanks for the ride, Dave.

By giving up my attachments, I was able to enjoy the race moment by moment. It rained or snowed on us almost the entire time. It was muddy, and sticky and awful, but we had the best time ever. We watched other racers fighting the same elements and issues have a terrible time and said, "Oh my god, they just don't see how much fun they're having!"

I took the lessons learned in the TransRockies race with me to the Baja 1000. Arriving in Mexico in preparation for the race, I was completely unattached to the outcome. I was just thrilled to be there and committed to do the best I could for the team.

When we become more aware of how the human mind works, we can see that our way of viewing the world is limited by our beliefs and current paradigms of thought. When we acknowledge this, we can break away from our existing limited mindset and invent any way of being and living that we want.

Racing my leg of the Baja 1000, I encountered challenge after dangerous challenge—miles of deep silt like baby powder, trails dotted in rocks the size of pumpkins, harrowing chases and near misses with buggies, extreme heat, brushes with death, running right into a herd of forty goats and shooting up a wall of rock to get around a race buggy in a full-on Batman-like maneuver.

When I reached mile marker 840, tired and bug-eyed, I started to hallucinate. I thought of Kelly and the kids waiting for me at the finish line, began getting emotional and realized my glutamine levels were dangerously low. I still needed to concentrate as I was travelling at over ninety miles an hour. There were lots of rocks, washouts and hidden dangers; I still had to be smart, because at that speed any small bubble in concentration could mean my life. I forced myself to treat it like meditation and focus on nothing but breathing and being. It worked!

About eleven hours after I took over (two more than I had planned and hydrated for, which explained the hallucinations), I rolled into my final pit and tagged out. In the end, we did finish in time. But, though I was happy with the outcome, the real win was the pure fun of it.

Days later, when I could walk again, I went for a run on the beach and, when I got to a picturesque spot, I stopped, looked out at the water and said, "So, what's next?"

A Baja racer once said, "If you knew you were making history you would have paid closer attention to it at the time." That's a great quote because you're doing just that, you're making history every day, in the big moments, like competing in crazy races, and in the little moments, when you share a precious moment with someone you love. No dream is too extreme when you are aware of your creative powers and responsibility—what will *you* dream extreme this year?

Darin Bullivant BA, BEd, is an author, speaker and the founder of Dare To Dream Extreme, a philanthropic organization geared at getting people out of their comfort zones (or ruts) and out there living their dreams, while at the same time raising awareness and funds for many different charities. He and his family have raised over twenty-two thousand dollars for The Children's Wish foundation and support several orphanages in Mexico and Cambodia. He is also a founding member of D.I.R.T. (the Dream It Race Team), which has competed successfully in many of the world's hardest races, including the Legendary Baja 1000, Xtinction Hard Enduro Race, Red Bull Rocks and Logs and the Trans-Rockies Mountain Bike Race.

A teacher of grades four, five and six in a Montessori classroom, Darin has been working with children for over twenty years. In his book The Things In Me *he teams up with his daughters, Hunter and Piper, and Mark Cromwell, an award-winning illustrator, to discuss awareness of emotions, fear and responsibility. He plans to expand the series to include topics on substance abuse, school bullying and other areas of concern. The primary goal is to open a dialogue between adults and kids regarding topics that can be difficult. Darin has developed a program geared at getting educators and parents to be effective communicators with their students and children.*

Darin is passionate about health and wellness and supports daily meditation, vegetarian diet and living a life of love and awareness. He is an advocate of Landmark Education and Peaks Potential personal growth companies as well as Centerpointe Research Institute and Holosync Meditation. He is also a VEGA ambassador and Juice Plus advocate. He hopes his story will inspire as many people as possible to live a life they love. His life's work is to make a difference. His new book, 24, features profiles of the twenty-four people who have inspired him the most and he will dedicate an hour to each of these people in his next extreme race, The 24 Hours of Adrenaline in Canmore, Alberta. To connect with Darin to help plan your next adventure, contribute to the Children's Wish Foundation, schedule an inspirational or educational speaking engagement, or to sponsor Darin directly, please contact him through www.DareToDreamExtreme.com.

Fabian Tan

FOR A LIVING CITY

The city was like a mouth with most of its teeth knocked out. I drove through it in the late dark night, the headlights of my rental car falling on block after block of doorless, windowless houses and empty streets. I saw a few people ducking around corners and moving in the gaping window spaces, but the seemingly deserted, gutted, foreclosed homes stretched for miles. Many of them looked as though they'd burned and the ones with people in them were otherwise indistinguishable from the abandoned ones.

Meanwhile, I was driving blind when I wasn't even used to driving on the right side of the road. In Singapore, we drive on the left. I had no GPS and nothing but a paper map from the gas station. Darkened streetlights, mazes of abandoned factories and industrial sites seemed to go on forever and then suddenly came to terrifying dead ends. *I am going to be killed,* I thought. *I was warned*—I'd taken out twice the normal amount of travel insurance, just in case. *This place is straight out of* Nightmare on Elm Street.

Detroit was a ghost town and I was freaking out. Singapore is very small. The whole country is almost exactly the same size as the city of Detroit. In case you do not know about Singapore, we are a lot like New York City, but as clean as Salt Lake City. We are a concrete jungle with skyscrapers all across the island state.

For six years my business has been in or near a metropolitan city almost free of crime. You can leave a car with keys in it and no one will drive it away. Singapore punishes a drug trafficker with the death penalty when in possession of heroin the size of a quarter. It canes those who vandalize or who are guilty of a sex offence. Suddenly, I had landed in the city everyone claims had the highest criminal offence rate in America, Detroit.

And I had come to invest in this urban disaster. In Singapore, our government was putting what we call "wet blankets" on the property sector, so my company had to look outside of the country for real estate deals. The common impression in Singapore is that American houses cost millions of dollars and the whole United States is like New York City. I heard you could buy a house in Detroit for thirty-five thousand dollars.

"No, you can get them for twenty thousand," Jeff told me.

Jeff is an American who lives in Singapore and is married to a Singaporean. He had been working for peanuts compared to what he had made as a plumber back home; I hired him as the plumbing

---

**Detroit was a ghost town and
I was freaking out.**

---

supervisor of my crew and paid him good money. Most of the Americans in Singapore were CEOs of banks and chief financial analysts, so at first he got a lot of teasing from the local guys; an American installing your water closet is a very interesting sight.

When Jeff confirmed the low home prices in Detroit, I thought, *Hell! Rent it out for six or eight hundred dollars, it gives you a fifteen percent yield!* In Singapore, when I get eight percent, my investors scream with joy. I'm taking them to the bank. So, a fifteen percent return, only thirty-five thousand dollars? Twenty thousand?

When I arrived in Detroit, it happened to be Thanksgiving. *No wonder none of the realtors I planned to meet are answering their phones.* I checked into a Red Roof Inn, recommended by Jeff, and stayed there for the next four days, while I waited for everyone's work lives to resume after the holiday. I drove around blindly with routes planned in my room. Not understanding the terms metro area, county and city, I just presumed all was Detroit. Some neighborhoods were nice, too: Waterford, Southfield, Dearborn, just to name a few. Only when I met the realtors did I learn the nicer neighborhoods were the suburbs.

The realtors I met with didn't even have to open doors for me to inspect the interiors of empty houses; the doors were nonexistent. But, it was also immediately obvious that there was huge potential. Most houses could be heavily rehabbed within four to six weeks; we could turn around whole blocks at a time and rent the houses at low rates to low-income people from the neighborhood. Affordable housing could begin to help create economic stability in the city.

If we could buy houses in bundles of fifty, or a hundred, or two hundred, we could make it worth our while: put a tenant in, sell the property at fifteen percent to the pool of investors and manage the property for them: A noble business model to house the homeless and create passive income for middle income investors. Never would anyone in Asia dream about owning a property for just thirty-five thousand American dollars, not to mention a net fifteen percent return, and have someone manage it for you.

As I got more educated and kept returning to Detroit, I realized we should buy homes in streets where, out of a block of twenty, maybe five or six houses were still in distress and other neighbors and organizations were also working to create a stable neighborhood. We bought those distressed places, turned them around and watched whole blocks suddenly bloom with color and life, with kids actually playing outside. We are now putting a hundred families a month into new homes people never imagined could be lived in again.

When I first arrived in Detroit, I saw nothing but trash. Then, beyond the trash, I saw the value of the houses. Finally, beyond the value of the houses, I saw the synergy of the people of Detroit trying to bring the city back to life. Communities were banding together to rehabilitate neighborhoods; nonprofit organizations were rebuilding schools and getting kids back into them. Community centers, urban agriculture, local businesses, new niche industries, many of them in green energy, were being created by local people.

Detroit is a diamond in the rough; a lot of people fail to see its beauty and possibility. Its potential is in its people. That's the beauty of Detroit—the resilience and ingenuity of its people, working together for change. And that's where the highest potential lies for its recovery. Though right now we're still dealing with

---

Detroit is a diamond in the rough.

---

seventy thousand empty houses in Detroit, though it looks from the outside like nothing but foreclosure and distress, many people in the neighborhoods are doing all they can to remove blight and revive their districts. While often people tend to complain about a problem, the people of Detroit are putting great energy into their city, working to solve these problems daily.

It would be foolish for us not to invest in these neighborhoods, not to step in and refurbish and repair the homes, help the neighborhoods gain back some pride and beauty and rent the homes to the people who live there at a price they can actually afford. We still make a good profit. Americans can buy the property cheaper, but the vast majority of investors are Asians, from overseas, who seek no surprises for the headaches of being a landlord. We bridge the impossible to become possible, investing in a location half the world away as though it was in the back yard.

Today, in the neighborhoods where we have paid thirty-five to forty thousand dollars for houses, home values go up to sixty thousand dollars. The growth is sustainable, not bubble-style. Our goal is to go deeper into Detroit and house ten thousand American families by 2020. But housing is only the first step and we're contributing to a lot of solutions. We know, too, that an industrial city can provide jobs to people with the lowest incomes. Industry is coming back to America and it's coming back to Detroit. We're supporting that growth, encouraging and investing in local people who are already doing specialized manufacturing.

People are terrified by crime rates in Detroit, but crime isn't a natural state. Crime comes with unemployment. When people have a place to live and a job, crime naturally goes down. In 2013, the crime rate in Detroit dropped dramatically, because the jobs started to return. People in the city are creating new niche industries and making millions, billions of dollars. They're putting money into medical research, green industries, rebuilding the city by creating jobs. This is only the beginning; the city has been so economically depressed, it will take another five to seven years to really see evidence of a recovery.

Every weekend I fly to a different part of Asia—Malaysia, Indonesia, Hong Kong, China—and give a talk to educate people about Detroit, about this American city that is fighting so hard to come back to life, while in so many ways it's been forgotten by the

Success is about being of service as a leader.

rest of the United States. My mission is to demonstrate the potential when you work on turning around a city with a whole coalition of passionate, hardworking people who share that mission.

It's powerful to look at our strengths and reflect on how they can help the world. My first leap was out of worry about money. The next generation is taken care of; now that I get to do what I want to do, I've made my second leap from financial freedom to abundance and giving back.

You become really successful only when your goals have the higher purpose of helping other people. If you are broke, it's pretty hard to find the energy to save the world. You're held back by money and all the problems it creates, like everybody in the rat race. But when you're finally able to break free from that cycle and make your life about a purpose, about service, the money flows in accordingly. When you go all out to help other people achieve something, rather than exploiting them, it creates real power.

When your motivation is service to people, life and work are fulfilling. They give you energy. You do what you love, because helping life flourish in this world is inexpressibly more fulfilling than making money. I sleep well, wake up early for the next day and don't get tired. My work is not a chore; I love what I do. If it was all about money, I would have stopped by now. Money as a motivation will always lead to a stopping point.

Success is about being of service as a leader and expanding, rather than contracting, communities' life forces. I'm so much more interested in helping communities and stabilizing neighborhoods in Detroit, and helping median-income people in Asia through such investments, than in the amount of money that can come in every month.

What gives me a sense of accomplishment is talking to people who live in the reclaimed, rehabilitated houses, seeing the smiles on their faces, their happiness with the neighborhoods, the houses, a sense of new possibility for the future. Best of all is seeing the pride they take in their own part of bringing life and joy back to Detroit, how they've worked together to create a living city from what was once only a nightmare. This is beautiful. This is joy.

Fabian Tan, born and raised in Singapore, is a real estate venture capitalist who specializes in value-added investment in real estate. Most recognized for his venture in Detroit, he has an aptitude for spotting opportunities and seeing beyond what others see. Having strong training in leadership, he has no qualms about taking his company from no employees to one hundred in two years. Living in financial abundance, Fabian seeks a higher purpose to serve the world with his strength, to help a thousand people achieve financial freedom and to help the city of Detroit regain its pride as the Motor City. Connect with Fabian at www.MidasDev.com.

Kathryn Cooper

NOWHERE TO GO BUT UP!

There goes my spine. I could be paralyzed, I thought—but quickly rejected the idea. Only moments earlier I had been working in one of the corrals on my family's farm, and now I was literally face down in the shit, being stomped nearly to death by a fourteen-hundred pound cow with a whole lot of attitude. I felt my bones breaking from the inside out and the pain throughout my entire body was intense and unimaginable.

I could hear horrible, primordial screaming and, knowing that my kids were in the next corral, I thought, *She's quit stomping me and now she's going after my kids.* My instinct to protect my kids shifted me through the shock of my injuries back into the moment; somehow I tracked the screaming and was shocked to discover it was coming from me.

I'd instinctively flipped onto my back and pulled my knees up to my chest because the pain was so great. That was all I could do, no matter how much adrenalin I had. I wasn't paralyzed, but I couldn't get up, though my mind cried out in fear that the crazy cow would return to finish me off any second. I just lay there in complete agony, knowing for the first time in my life that I couldn't summon all my strength and superwoman skills to get out of this.

Not long before the cow attack, I was living a good life—happily married for about twenty years; we had three wonderful kids and

I was looking after Grandpa in his golden years. We had two full-time businesses, with me managing operations of both and being hands-on at our over-six-hundred acre, one hundred and twenty head cattle farm. I also worked part-time in special needs education and still had my own coaching and training business—I wanted to do everything I could to make my dreams come true for myself and my family. Between all that and embracing daily family love, yoga, meditation and exercise to keep myself fit and strong, I had a pretty good balance.

My world came crashing down around me when my husband had a traumatic brain injury and the loving, gentle man I knew became a violent and confused stranger. Not only had I lost my life partner and all of his support in our life and family, but I also lost my business partner. I'd been given a one-way ticket to hell and my worst nightmare came true: I was left to do it all alone

I was overwhelmed by the sheer enormity of what I had to face—completely running on empty, I was praying for help every step of the way. My constant prayer for days was, *Please, God. Please just help me get through this, and then I'll take a rest and figure out what to do from there.* I was exhausted, and my own goals and dreams seemed very far away, even unattainable.

I was nearly killed right in front of them.

My children were ten, twelve and fourteen years old and I remember seeing the pain and confusion on their faces. Their world had completely turned upside down.

I sat them down and explained, "The doctors are doing everything they can to figure out what's happening." When I saw the fear in their eyes, I said, "I promise that whatever happens with your dad, I will always be there for you."

And a week later, I was nearly killed right in front of them. The cow was the proverbial straw that broke my back. Everything I'd been through in the last months brought me to the breaking point and I realized that I had nothing left—I was completely devastated and broken on every level: mind, body and spirit. The promise to my kids, "I will always be there for you," rang through my thoughts as I lay in the mud and muck of the corral. With my body broken and my life force bleeding away, I felt helpless, hopeless and completely overwhelmed with what life had given me.

"There is nowhere to go but up from here," said a voice in my head. My kids had already lost one parent; they would never get over losing both parents at the same time. Nobody would be there to look after my kids as I could. In that moment, I made a conscious decision to survive. I'd made a promise to my kids and somewhere I found a connection to the strength to do it for my kids when I couldn't do it for myself—I found my "why" to live.

I made a conscious decision to survive.

I was air-lifted to intensive care. All my ribs were broken and the cow had stomped my kidney and my spleen and broken part of the transverse process that runs along the spine. I now appreciate what a stroke patient with paralysis on one side might feel.

I overheard the doctor tell my family, in front of my kids, "You'd better say good-bye, because I don't think she's going to make it."

I'll never forget my terror that first night I was in the intensive care unit. Every time I moved I was engulfed in agony, even with the morphine they were giving me, and every breath I took was pure pain. All through the night, every time I'd drift off into a kind of drug-induced haze and pain-filled fog of sleep, I'd be awakened by the blood-curdling screaming and thrashings of a man on the other side of the curtain. My vitals must have been off the charts. I'd become terrified and I'd try to get out of the way, fearing the cow was coming to get me again.

One of the biggest risks I took was checking myself out of the hospital against the doctor's orders. He was adamant that I was still in tremendous pain and I could bleed out again, this time to death. Nevertheless, I needed to go home and look after my kids; nobody was there for them and when I talked to them on the phone, they were upset and acting out. I knew that, even if all I could do was lie on the couch or in bed, it would make a difference for them just to see that I was alive.

At home, I didn't have the luxury of nurses, spa tub baths or a button to press when the pain was too great. I thought I was doing better than I actually was and the illusion soon burst. Everything was an enormous effort—I couldn't even cook a meal. My kids became pretty good cooks after a while, because I would teach them from the couch and give them my recipes step-by-step.

We all worked together to do the basics; we forged deeper bonds; we all took baby steps together—and it was this slow process of learning that made me realize that if we were ever going to truly move forward, I needed to streamline our lives. Before

---

When you take action, nothing is impossible.

---

the incident, I'd been operating out of the pain and grief of losing a loved one. I'd operated out of the belief that, somehow, if I did enough and sacrificed enough, I could save my husband. What an eye-opener to realize that I wasn't ready to die to save him!

Now, I was operating from and motivated by my "why" in life. It gave me a clear vision of what I wanted to do and the courage and strength to do things for my children that I could not have done for myself. My "why" was giving my children a life in which they felt loved and safe and had a vision for success. I knew I might not have all the answers, but I could trust to take baby steps in life that would generate momentum and create success.

I began by changing the business model of how we ran our lives, putting new systems and targets in place—because I couldn't do everything hands-on myself. Daily, I made decisions about priorities and assets based on income, performance and equity and when it was clear to me what the next decision was, I made it. Learning how to do this took a lot of time and testing—I had to streamline my system for the most effective use of my time and energy, while minimizing my pain and maximizing my results.

This required ongoing adjustment as my abilities and health improved.

I also had to learn how to put myself first, to accept and receive help and support from others when appropriate. Having a network of support had a tremendous impact in my life when I couldn't do it for myself. It encouraged me and lifted some of the heaviness in my life to allow me to heal faster. I learned that I simply needed to receive and to accept that I was being looked after "Woman to Woman."

Other people's limitations and opinions do not have the power to limit what is possible in my life—unless I give them that power. I committed to doing anything and everything that I considered to be any way helpful to my recovery: I took control of my life and became innovative, proactive in my plan to create what I wanted; I set goals and did what I had to do to achieve them; I took baby steps every day; I received coaching and set up support when I needed it; sometimes I even took calculated risks for the bigger vision. Setting priorities within my new life vision helped. Learning to put myself first and then my children helped.

I realized that, if I didn't look after myself first, I wouldn't be there to look after anyone else. This pivotal realization helped me manage my time, energy and new priorities for the life and vision I wanted to create.

I started to live life in the sweet spot, the place where you are centered, balanced and living your life where nothing is impossible. The sweet spot is the place where you attain your personal and professional goals without sacrificing your family, sanity or health. It's where women of success are empowered to live, transform their lives and touch the lives of others.

When you take action, nothing is impossible. When a woman experiences more success in her life, no matter what her life circumstances are, her life balances and everything in her life changes for the better. As a woman, I've realized that my core service message in life is simple: Heart to Heart, Woman to Woman, Business to Business™.

Face down in the muck in the corral, thinking I was completely broken on all levels, feeling helpless and hopeless, I did not have a vision of my life the way it is today. I was merely concerned with survival and taking the next breath pain-free.

My life today has the momentum and flow of following my "why" in life. It's been amazing to connect with people all over the world, to have met and interviewed with some of the highest caliber of people such as Jack Welch, former CEO of General Electric; Randi Zuckerberg, former Director of Marketing & Development for Facebook; and Arnold Schwarzenegger. I was particularly thrilled to spend time with Steve Wozniak, co-founder of Apple Computers, when we celebrated our new i Coaching® business launch with Foxx Cooper i Coaching®.

Find your "why" in life—it will propel you beyond limitations and barriers and give you strength, courage, energy and vision beyond anything you will ever do just for yourself. Find your "why," and start taking those baby steps. Before long, you will realize that you've gone a lot farther than you ever thought possible. Go beyond possible, take action and nothing is impossible!

Kathryn Cooper empowers women entrepreneurs and business owners to more success in business and in life. "North America's Premier Women's Empowerment Authority," Kathryn is a number-one bestselling author; international speaker and trainer; a serial entrepreneur, CEO and founder of Women of Success, and Foxx Cooper i Coaching®.

Raised in poverty by her mother, who was a single parent with limited skills and employment prospects, Kathryn understood the value of dreaming big at a young age and further honed her life values to ensure integrity, clarity and focus. Commitment to a heart-centered life remains at the core of her every dream and goal. The traumatic brain injury of her husband and her own near-death shortly thereafter fueled Kathryn's decision to survive and to live her best successful life.

Kathryn has spent her career committed to helping thousands create powerful transformational learning experiences in business and life from the inside out. She shares her wisdom, experience and unique insights Heart to Heart, Woman to Woman, Business to Business™. She has spent the last decade empowering women all over the world to take ownership of their biggest dreams for their greatest success.

Through her Exhaustion to Empowered™ Women's Total Empowerment System, Kathryn helps overwhelmed and exhausted women attain their grandest personal and professional goals while enjoying a centered and balanced success life. She is the creator of the ReStructure Your Mindset TTA Blueprint for Success™ Series, the Ready...Set...Go... 30-Day Quick Start to Success™ Program and the TTA Blueprint™, a step-by-step tool that empowers women to transition, transform and attain their personal goals and professional ambitions. Come and play in Kathryn's success resources at www.KathrynCooperLive.com and connect with her at www. WomenofSuccess.com.

Peter Thompson Moles

RESOLUTION FOR REINVENTION

I was on the treadmill at my health club, watching CNN when it happened: The name of my former employer—First Commodity Corporation of Boston (FCCB)—flashed across the screen, followed by pictures of the FBI walking into their corporate offices. Startled, I stared, my eyes glued to the screen, as CNN listed the names of many brokers under indictment.

Although I was not a trader and did not make any transactions while employed at FCCB, I braced myself. I had been their top-producing fundraiser during the few years I worked for the company. I had heard the rumors that people were going down on Wall Street and about the Illinois District Attorney who wanted to make his mark by going after the Chicago-based brokers, but it never occurred to me that they would come gunning for me.

The first year I sold something I was named "Salesman of the Year." FCCB bestowed this honor on me after I had raised more than one million dollars in speculative commodity capital. It was 1981. I was twenty-one years old and I did all of this over the telephone. I never met a customer in person.

The markets peaked in 1979, when gold sold for over eight-hundred dollars an ounce. The downward spiral had begun in the markets and the high-flying, reckless investment whirl of the 1980s was set to begin. Over the next few years, I went on to achieve "Salesman of the Year" several times and was picked to open an office in Mountainview, California in 1985. I returned to Chicago to work for another commodity company in 1986.

As happened to many others, on October 19, 1987—known as Black Monday because of the drastic meltdown of the markets— FCCB and everyone who worked there, including me, lost everything in their portfolios. But that was not the worst of it.

Now, watching the names of more than a hundred targeted brokers flash across the television screen, my heart raced. And then there it was—my own name, listed among those under indictment. Until that moment, I had no idea I was under investigation. Numb with shock, I was overwhelmed with instant humiliation and embarrassment. *Everyone will see this,* I thought, *my family, my wife, my neighbors.* I was overwhelmed—but it was only the beginning of months of hell.

On January 18, 1989, I stood before a federal judge in a Chicago courtroom, which was empty except for my public defender, a district attorney, a court stenographer and my mother. I was charged with mail fraud, wire fraud and racketeering, for which the minimum sentence in Illinois is twenty-six years of incarceration.

I had no idea I was under investigation.

It was mind-blowing. My entire life had fallen apart, all because I had raised money for brokers during the high-flying times portrayed in the film *The Wolf of Wall Street.*

I was broke and had nothing left. I agreed to plead guilty to one count of wire fraud and pledged to cooperate in the feds' ongoing investigation. This was a felony charge. I was married with three small children. *How would I provide for my family as a convicted felon?*

Because I cooperated, the authorities realized I was not the trader involved, but had just raised the capital. My penalty was light: a thirty thousand dollar fine and a four-month sentence with work release. Still, the fall from grace hit me hard. I was paralyzed, emotionally and mentally frozen. I felt like a pinball machine on tilt—the lights were blinking, but nothing was happening.

Fortunately, the paralysis didn't last long. Even at the young age of twenty-eight, I was already practiced in the teachings of great transformational leaders. I was weaned on Norman Vincent Peale—my mother handed me a copy of *The Power of Positive Thinking* when I was just a kid. My very first day on the job at FCCB, I was handed a copy of Napoleon Hill's *Think and Grow Rich* and my life was forever changed. The power of sales was cemented in my core.

Each day on the job I had been spoon-fed key principles—believe, conceive, achieve. I learned to eat rejection for breakfast. My success in sales was directly related to my obsessive desire to understand, not just Napoleon Hill's manifesto, but also all of the great sales prophets, from Brian Tracy to Zig Ziglar. Between that training and my mother's efforts to instill the values of our ancestors—the survivors and trailblazers of our family tree—within me, I was able to pick myself up quickly.

With a family to provide for, I reached deep into the gospel of *Think and Grow Rich* and found comfort and wise counsel: "With every adversity comes the seed of an equivalent or greater benefit."

I made a resolution for reinvention. As I had done for years when setting my sales goals, I created a mission statement for change, detailing exactly what I wanted to see happen in a specific period of time and what I was willing to sacrifice to get it. I repeated my mission statement at least ten times a day, each time fortifying the force field around me that blocked negativity and naysayers and provided me with a powerful ability to weather any storm, to meet any challenge. I created a new vision for my life and committed to a daily practice of renewal to realize that vision.

In 1990, a former commodities colleague phoned to introduce me to the world of merchant payment processing. Peachtree Bankcard's headquarters was housed in an impressively tall, marble building. As I entered, I could feel great possibility surge through me.

When they offered me the job, I said, "I love it. I'll start January fifteenth." My mission statement was coming to fruition, as I knew it would.

Peachtree was just launching a check guarantee product that complemented the credit card processing accounts. I applied my formula for sales and an early version of the Thompson Techniques—every bit of knowledge I had accumulated over the

---

I created a mantra for change.

---

years and every single strategy I had proven. Within two weeks, I closed twenty-four accounts.

Then, Peachtree's vice president said the CEO would like to see me. Still dealing with the wounds and results of my indictment, I felt anxious and uneasy sitting in the anteroom of the CEO's office. My mind raced. *Uh-oh, what have I done? Am I in trouble?*

Inside his office, the CEO, who also owned Cherry Payment Systems, Inc., sat behind his huge mahogany desk, twirling a large brass letter opener and playing with his suspenders. Finally, he said, "Peter, I like the way you make things simple. We have an opportunity for you."

He and Peachtree's vice president led me to the tenth floor, to a large, raw space that was not yet built out.

The CEO said, "I know you come from phone sales. You've demonstrated that you can take a product you hardly know and sell the heck out of it. Can you build a one hundred and twenty person phone room and teach them to sell both our check service and our credit card service?"

This took my breath away. In just two short weeks, my mission statement, my commitment to daily renewal and my proven sales strategy had landed me just the opportunity I needed to completely reinvent myself. Without hesitation I said, "Yes."

It took six months to populate the room and, further, to open thirty satellite offices in the Midwest. I was named Vice President Sales Midwest for Cherry Payment. The region spanned from

Minneapolis to New Orleans and from Omaha to Cleveland. We grew to four hundred new accounts weekly in those first six months. Then, the company was sold to investment banking firm William Blair in the early 1990s and I was starting over. Again. From the sales greats, I knew that "tough times never last, tough people do."

So I made another resolution for reinvention. This time, I would start my own company. Over the next few years I fixated on staying in the game. I worked the principles, I used my mantra and I had a big "why" behind the mindset programming I used to reinvent myself yet again. With this strategy, I was able to meet goals others would deem "impossible." I had a white-hot desire to succeed and that, combined with my evolving Thompson Techniques, was like nitroglycerine.

After building and selling two successful merchant services companies, I incorporated The Merchant Source, which focuses on face-to-face, consultative selling. We went from zero to eighty million dollars in monthly processing in five years. Building a sales

For me, impossible isn't a reality.

group using Thompson Techniques' tenets, I trained hundreds of independent agents. Today, my company provides me with a seven-figure, massive passive residual annual income, thanks to residuals generated by about a hundred agents, thirty whom produce processing volume of more than six hundred million annually. The top producers each earn between three hundred thousand and seven hundred thousand dollars annually in residuals and commissions on direct sales using the Thompson Techniques.

You may not have had to overcome a fall from grace on the same level I experienced, or at all, but each and every one of us will be tasked with facing challenges and changes that require us to reinvent ourselves. This is the age we live in. Whether it's because of a health crisis, a merger acquisition, downsizing, a change in technology or a desire to break through to the next level, we will all have to continue to mold and adapt ourselves to new circumstances.

Gone are the days of working thirty years at the same company, earning your watch and retiring with enough money for a respectable life. I think you know that all too well and I think that, like me, you want more. You're not interested in a job that limits your ability to earn, to invent, to achieve, to grow. You want to *create* without limits.

In 2011, I began putting together the strategy to take the Thompson Techniques global after experiencing extreme fatigue and a misdiagnosis. Wings of angels carried me through a tough year that ended in lifesaving heart by-pass surgery, which became my new, driving "why" and cemented in me the desire to go global.

For me, daily renewal was and remains an obsession. It's as though I'm a mutant from the *X-Men* series and my superpower is reinvention. Every day I repeat my mantra over and over again: Motivation by obsession. Obsession for love. Love for enthusiasm. Enthusiasm created by strategy. Strategy to ensure Health, Happiness and Freedom. M-O-L-E-S.

If you're not obsessed with motivation, you're not going to get out of bed, much less accomplish your four positive moneymaking actions every day. If you don't have love in your heart at every moment of every day, you could turn down the wrong road and create a win-lose scenario that might make you money today, but won't make you wealthy in the long run. Enthusiasm is what brought good people to this great country and fostered the entrepreneurial spirit that inspires all of us to pursue the Great American Dream. Strategy is absolutely essential for anyone in pursuit of any goal, large or small. In the Thompson Techniques, I share the three keys of the tripod for success: the "Road to Massive Passive Residual Income," the "Seven Easy Steps to Life Transformation" and "Empowering Your "'Why.'" Everyone needs to know how to close, whether you're selling merchant services over the phone or pitching an idea to an investor—even if you're trying to convince your family to get on board with your dream.

We all need to learn how to "get the sale" and seal the deal quickly, over and over again.

For me, impossible isn't a reality. There is nothing that cannot be achieved—and that's true for you, too. You may not be standing on a treadmill when your life takes a turn you did not expect; you may not have to face federal prosecution and public humiliation. But I know your challenges are very real. You are either living or dying and, no matter what you come up against, today is not your day to die. Know that you, too, can come back from whatever hell you've experienced. You *can* break through to the next level. I'm no hero; my process can be duplicated.

Create your own sunrise. Begin each day as if it is the first day of your life and live it as if it's the last. Do not hold back. There is no failure. See yourself crossing that finish line before it even exists. Foster that white-hot desire and commit to a daily renewal. When you follow a simple process like the tripod I developed for my own reinvention, winning is inevitable.

Peter Thompson Moles is a life transformation expert. Author, speaker and coach, he founded Thompson Technique, Inc., a success education and motivational company designed to inspire people to achieve their dreams. After more than thirty years as a top performer in sales, building many successful teams in the brokerage and merchant service industries, Peter created the Thompson Techniques, his proven training and motivating approach that incorporates the collective knowledge of the great modern day sales teachers and motivators with his own best sales-closing strategies. The Thompson Techniques are so effective that even average, order-taking sales reps who are motivated to learn and dream can be converted into top-echelon master closers.

Peter began his sales career in 1980, at age twenty, when he joined First Commodity Corporation of Boston (FCCB), based in Chicago. In this job, he raised capital from investors over the telephone for commodity brokers to invest. In his first full year, Peter raised more than a million dollars in speculative commodity capital, was named "Salesman of the Year" and was later tasked with hiring and training for a new branch sales office.

After leaving FCCB, Peter worked for several financial corporations and, in 1991, joined Peachtree Bankcard and began his twenty-three year run in merchant payment services. At Peachtree, he built a one hundred and twenty person phone room and opened thirty Midwest satellite offices, which, in turn, opened four hundred new accounts weekly in their first six months. He was named Vice President Sales Midwest at an affiliated company, directing sales operations from Minneapolis to New Orleans and from Omaha to Cleveland. He left Peachtree in 1993, when the company was sold.

Peter went on to launch three merchant services companies that each grew from three hundred to four hundred new accounts per month; he sold two of the companies. In 2007, Peter incorporated his current company, The Merchant Source, which specializes in face-to-face consultative selling to merchants. Under his guidance and following the Thompson Techniques, The Merchant Source grew from zero to eighty million dollars in monthly processing in just five years. During his thirty-four year run in the direct sales industry, he has been directly responsible for raising over one hundred million dollars in investment capital and for opening more than fifty thousand merchant accounts.

Currently writing a book on his powerful transformational strategies, Peter offers in-person training in the Thompson Techniques at his Millionaire Mason Blueprint Courses. To connect with Peter, visit www.ThompsonTechniques.com.

Rhonda Spinks

PASS THE TORCH

When it comes to living a successful life, people often use the metaphor of running a race. You train hard; you exert all your energy; you visualize reaching the finish line; you push and concentrate and strive with every cell of your being and then—you win! But what do you win, when the victory is only for yourself? What do you truly gain? I believe that this life is actually a relay race, not some solo sprint to win for the sake of your own glory. You've got to run a great race—not just for yourself, but so you can pass the torch to the next runner.

In 2009, I was zestfully racing through my own busy life. I was in my early thirties, newly married and juggling a lot. I was serving in the Army National Guard, teaching at Tulsa Community College, pursuing my master's degree, volunteering at the United States Fish and Wildlife Service and being very actively involved in my local church. I was in peak physical condition and felt great. When I had a lump in my breast checked out, the last thing I expected was bad news.

A funny thing about being human is that feeling of invincibility you have up until the moment of death. It's universal. You don't want to live in a state of fear, but living without awareness of your own mortality doesn't exactly help you live your life on purpose. It produces an undercurrent in your life, a voice that whispers,

I'll always have more time. Nothing to worry about. That's what I was thinking even as my husband, Matt, and I joked in the clinic waiting room. I was totally fine, totally healthy. We weren't really worried; this was the first of a series of errands. The grocery store was next. Still, Matt was with me, holding my hand when the doctor walked in to tell us the test results.

"I'm so sorry," he said. "The test results show cancer. It's very serious. Stage 3."

I felt Matt squeeze my hand. I couldn't speak. I turned to look at him and saw tears rolling down his face. My whole body was numb. *CANCER!* The word alone sent waves of horror through me. *How could this be? What have I done to deserve this? How could my body betray me like this—I thought I was fine! Cancer? That means coughing up blood; it means hair falling out. It means I'm dead. He's pronounced my death sentence.*

I could understand nothing the doctor said after hearing the word *cancer*. It was all a blur. Instead, I heard the vows Matt had made only six months ago, heard his deep voice saying, "In sickness and in health."

I wanted to scream. *Already? You already want to put him to the test?*

The test results show cancer.

Later, Matt had to tell me the rest of what the doctor had said: "It has spread into the lymph nodes of your arm. We'll have to do surgery right away. Mastectomy. Then a course of chemotherapy. Radiation. Nine months of treatment."

I just stared. I didn't cry. I was numb. We walked out of the clinic as if emerging from a bombed building. "Okay," I said briskly to Matt, "so, we're going to the grocery store now."

He gave me a brief, searching look, then nodded and smiled. "Okay, love. Let's go wherever you want."

I was aware enough for that flicker of his expression to break my heart. I was trying to act normal, so he would too.

As we walked into the store and past the enormous piles of onions and potatoes, I got the strangest feeling: *Can all these people, floating around in their normal everyday lives, see the brand on my forehead:* diseased, quarantined, dying? I felt so exposed. I turned and said desperately to Matt, "Oh, no. We've got to get out of here. We have to go."

I came home that day thinking I might as well fold my arms and be placed in a casket. Even as a Christian, it was hard for me to express a prayer. But, I was led to get up and call my pastors.

I put them on speaker-phone, listening with Matt while they ministered to us. They said, "This is just a diagnosis, not a death sentence."

Have I blessed anyone in this life?

The words stirred me deeply. Instinctively, I felt it was true. *Get your focus back on, girl. You have a life to live. Chemo, whatever, just get through the treatments.*

Right away, I decided I couldn't afford to fall apart. I didn't want anything to be different. *I'll make it. I'll make it.* During treatment, no one but my husband had any idea I had cancer. Not even my family—I didn't want them to worry and I didn't want them to see me as weak. And I was not weak. Even though my body was telling me differently, I went into *warrior* mode. I was determined to fight this and be back to normal.

After the mastectomy, I could barely lift my arm and, when I had to write exclusively on the bottom quarter of the blackboard during classes, I didn't divulge any of the details to my students. I just told them my arm hurt.

The warrior approach worked until after my first chemotherapy appointment. It's hard to stay strong when your body feels as though it's aged forty years. That first round of chemo knocked me flat for a few days. I felt so weak. My nail beds became black and so did my urine. My hair started falling out. The reality of the toxicity of the treatment I was taking set in. The nurses even instructed me to sterilize the toilet after each use. I felt like a walking bag of poison—a bio-hazard. *If this is just the beginning, how will I survive?*

Waiting in my doctor's examination room a few days later, so weak, I started asking myself more questions I hadn't wanted to face—questions people ask themselves only at the end of their lives: *Have I really lived? What kind of a life have I lived? Have I blessed anyone in this life? When I'm gone, will anyone remember me? Have I made a difference? Oh, God, please give me a second chance at answering these questions! Please give me the strength to keep going! Please help me not to give up!*

Just then, I looked up and noticed a picture on the wall. Maybe it had been there all along, but I was noticing it now for the first time. It was a photo of Joel Bacal, one of my doctor's former patients, a cancer survivor who raced trucks for sport. There he was in the cab of his truck, full-faced, full head of hair, looking happy and healthy. The script below read, "Thanks for giving me a second chance at life!"

It was exactly what I needed to see. It was the answer to my prayers. Here was someone who had gone through the same horrible treatment and had had the feelings I was experiencing and he *made it.* He was free to pursue his life, his dreams; he was better, back to normal. *Healthy,* even! Not just not dead. I felt a huge swell of hope. *I can't give up!* My mind was suddenly flooded with all the things I had dreamed of doing one day, with my husband and for myself, things I wanted to learn and give, everything I had so nonchalantly put off to do later. *I still have a God-given purpose to fulfill!*

Suddenly, I felt stronger than I had in months. And it hit me: *All this came from the power of a testimony—from a simple picture that told a story of triumph over what I was struggling with.* Without even knowing it, Joel told me his story through that one picture.

I saw an even bigger glimmer of hope. *Could my story also inspire someone else who will be going through this experience?* The answer was a resounding "yes!" Joel's win inspired me, and my win could inspire someone else. Now, it was on! It was no longer about just winning for me, but also for those coming after me. I saw what my true destiny is: to leave a legacy for the next generation. If this is what Joel's story could do to change my life, how could my own story give hope to others? *It's not enough to win. I have to pass on the torch of hope to the next runner.*

From that point on, my ambition has been to inspire others. I do this by telling my story. We all go through crazy stuff in life; it's inevitable. I realized from this experience it's not about what you go through as much as about how you chose to go through it. The most powerful thing we have in this life is our God-given ability to choose. If you choose to live your life with your end purpose in

---

Now the baton has been passed to us.

---

mind, I'm convinced you will ultimately end up being a blessing to those coming after you.

The great movers, shakers and world changers of the past, whose lives purchased the freedoms and benefits we have today, were those who dared to fully live, fight and push through their tough times, struggles and temptations to quit. They were willing to stick in there and overcome even when circumstances were hard and everything wasn't in their favor, believing that their struggles would one day pay off. Our history books now tell their story— their testimonies.

Now the baton has been passed to us. What are we going to do in our leg of the race of life? What significant things are we going to pass on to the generations coming after us? Will we propel them forward or set them back?

We owe it to the next generation to live our lives to the fullest and to fight for a better life for them. None of us should leave this life without leaving something positive to pass on! And we should never underestimate the power of our stories.

Today, I've been cancer-free for almost five years. I have had reconstructive surgery after the mastectomy. I went on to earn my master's degree and I am now training for figure bodybuilding competitions. Cancer has got nothing on me! I'm fitter than I've ever been. Sometimes I do not want to train. But I keep in mind what my perseverance and victory could mean for somebody else one day—my daughter, granddaughter, anyone facing a challenge. I might not know that person, just as Joel the truck racer will never know how profoundly his action changed my life; I know that—now that I've embraced it—my own story will have its own ripple effect.

Whatever your story is, I encourage you to tell it—not just the wins, but also the struggles you went through to attain them. Don't downplay or discredit it; you never know who needs to hear it. People are depending on you. We take our own stories for granted, but what if we didn't have them? What if I'd never heard of anybody surviving cancer? What would make me think I could?

At the end of your life, you want to know that you've left something behind to bless the world. Life is a relay race. Let's live each day on purpose, so we can pass the torch.

Rhonda Spinks was born in Boston, MA, and grew up in Trinidad, West Indies. She returned to the United States to attend college in Oklahoma and has remained there. A transformational speaker, coach and author, Rhonda also works for the United States Fish and Wildlife Service as a wildlife biologist and serves as a Captain in the Army National Guard. Check out Rhonda's YouTube channel, "You Call the Shots," and connect with her at www.YouCallTheShots.net.

Walter Anderson

ONE STEP AT A TIME

The air is very thin and cold at 18,341 feet above sea level. One thousand feet from the summit of Mount Kilimanjaro, the highest freestanding mountain in the world, my mind began to panic. *I can't breathe. I'm dying. I need oxygen.* Surrounded by pitch-black darkness and blizzard conditions, I started to hyperventilate. My heart felt like it was beating outside of my chest. *This is ridiculous! What am I doing up here? Why do people do this?*

Despite months of training, climbing through five climate zones in seven days with temperatures ranging from 104 degrees Fahrenheit down to -15 degrees Fahrenheit, overcoming obstacles and challenges and pushing past my fears, all I wanted to do was turn around and go back down the mountain. It would take courage and every tool in my "toolbox" to get me up the last thousand feet.

I've always had the desire to climb mountains. (I still have Mount Everest on my bucket list.) The opportunity to climb Mount Kilimanjaro came at a time in my life when I had achieved success in business, reaching the top of the ladder in my market niche. I was ready for a great adventure.

While hiking, my friend Stephen had mentioned that he was planning to climb Mount Kilimanjaro. Something inside told me I was meant to join him. I said, "I've always wanted to go to Africa and climb Mount Kilimanjaro. Do you mind if I come along?"

Stephen agreed and together with another friend, Jeff, we prepared to climb the mountain.

The long climb up the "Mountain of Greatness" was a remarkable journey. From walking through hot, dry African bush lands, where herds of elephants roam, to hiking through humid jungles where monkeys chattered and exotic birds chirruped, to slogging through pungent bogs and eerie swamps, where the mountain's mist closed in around us to zero visibility, and finally to Arctic conditions, where glistening walls of blue ice four-stories thick mark the edge of ancient glaciers millions and millions of years old, each moment offered a stunning example of nature's power, every day a new life lesson.

In addition to the three of us, our group of twelve consisted of three porters for each climber, two guides and one cook. Our main guide, a man who had helped other climbers reach the summit 175 times, taught me a fundamental lesson for achieving any goal. It is a simple Swahili phrase, *pole-pole* (pole-ay pole-ay), which means "slowly, slowly" or "take it easy, never mind." He explained that *pole-pole* was the only way we would make it all the way up the mountain, one step at a time, as a slow ascent would allow our bodies to acclimate to the altitude. All day long, we would take

---

Each moment offered a stunning example of nature's power.

---

a step, breathe, take another step, breathe, step, breathe, step, breathe, our bodies getting used to the thin air. One step at a time, one breath at a time; keep moving, keep climbing. *Pole-pole, pole-pole.*

Trying to climb your own mountain as fast as you can, whether it's an actual mountain like Kilimanjaro, a career or business aspiration, a fitness transformation or a relationship goal, will only exhaust you and might derail your journey altogether. Likewise, focusing solely on the end goal, rather than on your next steps, can leave you feeling overwhelmed, so that you concede to your own doubts and give up altogether. Success, like any major goal, is like climbing a mountain. You do it one step at a time. You can imagine what the view from the summit looks like and what it will feel like when you get there, but you still have to take the next step. Let your vision pull you in the right direction, but just keep moving. When you take small steps consistently, over time you achieve extraordinary results. It's in the momentum. Step, breathe, step, breathe, step, breathe.

Climbing the mountain, I also learned the importance of choosing my path wisely. We make many choices in life; the right choices lead to success. As I explained, climbing to 19,341 feet is a process of acclimating to the altitude, which is why the process

You go up; you come down and you rest.

involves not only going up, but also coming back down to rest until you're ready to try again. You go up; you come down and you rest. You go up; you come down and you rest. This is the correct "path" for reaching the summit.

Well into our journey and climbing in high altitudes, we reached a deep crevice with switchbacks all the way down and up again. At the same time, Jeff noticed a path that went straight up to our next camp and said, "I'm going to run right up there, and I'll be drinking tea when you get there."

One of the porters shook his head and said, "*Pole-pole.*"

When we agreed with the porter, Jeff said, "I've been up here enough days now. I feel strong and healthy and I'm younger than you guys. I'm going to do it anyway." Jeff disappeared up the mountain and the rest of our group followed the switchbacks, the correct path.

We arrived at camp several hours later to find Jeff very ill. Altitude sickness is quite painful; the only cure for it is going back down to lower elevations. Fortunately, Jeff was able to build up his fluids and get going, but his choice slowed down the hike. When we choose to turn away from our guides and not follow the correct path to our goal in order to accelerate things, we risk harming ourselves—and failing completely. Follow the path laid out before you and take the necessary steps to achieve your goal. At times, you may feel as though you're taking two steps backward, but if you take a rest and then keep moving, you'll get there.

Many years in business and more than a decade of study with some of the world's most renowned thought leaders on the principles of success had taught me to trust my instincts, so it wasn't so much a new lesson learned on the mountain that week,

In almost every case, the right choice is your gut feeling.

but an affirmation that going with my gut is absolutely critical in the pursuit of any goal.

One morning, while getting ready to set out, I had a feeling that I should put on my gaiters, protective covers worn over the boot and lower pants leg. When my friends and the other climbers noticed me putting them on, I said, "I have a hunch we're going to encounter some swampland today and get soaking wet."

The other guys said, "You don't need your gaiters. The weather has been dry. It's not going to happen."

I disagreed at first, but then caved and agreed and took them off. Sure enough, later that day we ran right into bog and ended up soaked up to our knees. Our boots and socks got muddy; the rest of the hike was uncomfortable and we got blisters. *I should have listened. My feet would be warm and dry.*

In almost every case, the right choice is your gut feeling. When you allow other voices—the voices in your head, causing you to doubt yourself and the voices of others who disagree with you—to sway you from making the correct decisions for yourself, reaching the summit becomes next to impossible. How can you succeed if you let others choose your path or stop you from moving at all?

It's important to tune in to your intuition. Sometimes you experience it as a slight vibration, a pull, a heartbeat. Your instinct is your internal compass; I believe it exists in our chests and our hearts and sometimes in our stomachs. It could be as subtle as a whisper, as slight as a butterfly wing, or something that bends you over with realization. All of a sudden, you know something is ending, or coming, or something needs to change. We all have these instincts and, as you become more aware of yours, you will be able to tune in to them like a radio.

When internal mental chatter influences you away from your gut feelings, it's really just your mind trying to protect you from harm. In this way, we are caving to a fearful mindset. When I experience this, I try to acknowledge the unwelcome thoughts and follow through despite my mind's conflict. *Thank you for sharing. I understand. Never mind, I'm moving on now.*

My mantra as we continued our climb up the mountain was: *Don't think, don't think, don't think.* When it came to failing or succeeding in the climb, understanding and applying these three life lessons—"slowly, slowly, one step at a time," choose the right path and trust your instincts—made all the difference.

On the final evening of our climb, our guide awakened us at midnight. The stars were as thick and creamy as milk; at high altitude, it's as if you can reach out and scoop up a handful of them to place in your pocket. With only a tiny headlamp to guide me and the boots of the climber visible in front of me, I began the final stage of the ascent.

And there I gave in to the panic of my mind. One thousand feet from the summit, breathing with fifty percent less oxygen, I was sure I would die if I didn't turn around and go back down the mountain. So I stopped. I took a breath. I reminded myself that my body was capable of finishing the climb and that because I had not experienced these challenges before, my mind was simply trying to take me out. To succeed, I needed to let go of the limitations presented by my mind-chatter. I got back into my body, let go of my fear and returned to what I learned. *Slowly, slowly, take it easy, never mind. One step at a time. Stay on the right path. Don't think, don't think, don't think.*

After many hours of placing one foot in front of the other—*pole-pole, step, breathe, step, breathe, pole-pole*—the frozen darkness gave way to shades of gray, until faint outlines of peaks and clouds formed. Slowly, color started to flow in like a water-color painting, as if the creator was splashing the sky with the broad strokes of his brush.

Finally, as we reached the crumbling crest of the volcano's crater, I turned around and experienced the magnificent breathtaking beauty of the first rays of sun dancing over and around the clouds and mountain peaks in an explosion of color and light. My heart pounded as tears streamed down my face, instantly turning to ice. I was in awe as I witnessed the creation of a new day. In that moment, I knew: *I can accomplish anything, as long as I put my mind to it. No longer will limiting beliefs hold me back. Everything I have learned up until now has prepared me for this moment."*

The process of attaining a goal is difficult, but anything is possible if you follow your heart and get out of your head.

Training for success takes months and months of preparation, starting with the smallest things. In training for my climb up Mount Kilimanjaro, running up and down two hundred flights of stairs until I could do it without stopping was my first "small thing." Yours could be making that phone call, taking that class, saying "yes." Whatever your next step is, do it. Then check it off the list and take the next step. Slowly, slowly. Breathe. Step. Breathe. Step. Breathe. Step.

It has been said that life begins at the edge of your comfort zone. When you get that nervous feeling, whether it's just goose bumps or full-blown panic, that's when you know your life is about to change. Most of us retract when this happens; we choose to climb down our own mountain and sit it out. But, if you can just focus on the next step and the next, letting go of the fearful messages of the mind, and slowly, slowly ascend on your correct path, you will acclimate to new comfort zones, climbing higher and higher still until you reach the summit of your dreams.

WALTER ANDERSON

Walter Anderson is a speaker, author and trainer on a mission to lead, inspire and motivate others to achieve their goals. Well-known for his high energy and enthusiasm, Walter helps people create positive change through his keynotes, books and coaching. An information systems entrepreneur and business owner with more than twenty years' experience in business, he knows that success is a result of keeping businesses customer-focused and building relationships based on outstanding service. Walter is the past president of the Greater Nanaimo Chamber of Commerce as well as past president of the Nanaimo Oceanside Rotary Club. Connect with Walter at www. WalterAnderson.ca.

Denice Young

PASSION IGNITING

It was pandemonium. Before my eyes, the vast space was filled with rows and rows of cots, some occupied, many still waiting for the thousands who were on their way. A group of people walked by with wet marks up to their shoulders from wading through water that almost reached their mouths. I still remember their faces—they looked as if they had lost hope. It was like a scene from a disaster movie! Except it wasn't a movie—it was as real as it gets.

It was September 2005 and I was standing on a huge ramp leading down into the Houston Astrodome. Some twenty-five thousand Hurricane Katrina survivors were being bused from the Superdome in New Orleans, where they had spent the last five to seven days in dramatic and ever-worsening conditions. I was there as one of the many volunteers who came to help in any way we could. The scene before me put my own frustrations into perspective very quickly.

For the past fifteen years, I had been a successful entrepreneur, working for big multinational companies, including IBM, Hewlett-Packard and Sony, and making good money, but I wasn't really excited about going to work every day. Like so many of us, I was doing something I was good at, but I didn't really have passion for the work. Something was missing. Mr. Les Brown, the world-renowned motivational speaker, encouraged me to find my true calling, the thing I wanted to bring to the world. I had heard him speak several years before and thought, *This is something I could be doing.*

Because of my background as a Certified Public Accountant and my natural talent for speaking, I decided to dedicate myself to helping others live more healthy and wealthy lives by teaching them to tend to those resources that were placed in their hands. It seemed a logical choice.

Les Brown became my mentor. I did some traveling with him, speaking on stages across the country. I created two programs of financial empowerment, called "You Deserve To Be Rich" and "Attacking The Credit Monster," and I began to sell them to eager audiences. And yet, I still didn't feel that deep conviction that I'm at the right place, doing the right things for the right reason.

My primary goal was to make an impact and I did not see that happening, at least not quickly enough for me. I was ready to give up the whole financial empowerment focus should some other calling reveal itself.

Then my friend Tonya announced that she was moving to Dallas, Texas and I thought, *Why not? Maybe I need a change of place.* So I left behind my beloved adopted home city of Los Angeles, California and went with her—not for a job, or a relationship, or any other rational reason.

You know how sometimes it's time to move from one station in life to another, from one set of circumstances to a new one, and it's like divine intervention that causes you to be in a certain spot at a certain time? I'm not sure I would have been in the Astrodome helping those people if I hadn't lived in Dallas then. After all, so often when you watch tragedies in faraway places, like the tsunami in Indonesia, you can't do much more than call the Red Cross and make a donation.

One morning a month after our move, Tonya came into my room and declared, "They need hugs!"

I wasn't fully awake yet. "Who needs hugs? What are you talking about?" I asked, confused.

"There's a minister on TV," she explained, "saying that the people coming from New Orleans are gonna need food, clothes and shelter, but most of all, they're gonna need hugs. They're gonna need someone to tell them that it's gonna be okay and that they can get through this and they're gonna need hugs. We can do hugs."

I thought about it for a second and said, "Yeah, we can do hugs."

We left immediately. With only a few changes of clothes and without so much as securing a hotel room, we drove to Houston and went right to the Reliant Center—and were promptly sent away. The first buses had not arrived; the Red Cross people at the gate told us to return in the morning. So it wasn't until the next day that I first stood on that ramp, looking at the sea of people

It was like a scene from a disaster movie! Except it wasn't a movie.

connected by the common tragedy. I didn't know then that the next ten days spent helping them would help me in ways I never expected.

Our first assignment was triage. Many survivors needed medical attention and our job was to determine who needed urgent care and who could wait. We asked questions and took notes and soon it became apparent that, while some patients were in pain or serious distress, many simply needed new prescriptions filled. They were people with diabetes, asthma, high blood pressure—all kinds of chronic conditions—who'd left their homes in such a hurry that they had left their medications.

Five hours later, we were moved to clothes distribution. While sorting the meager amount of clothes we had at our disposal at the beginning and handing them out to those in need, we had a chance to talk to a lot of people. The more we saw and heard, the more we understood just how dramatic the situation of the New Orleans survivors had been.

I remember an elderly woman in a wheelchair. She could have been around eighty. Her feet were wet, so I offered to put dry socks on her, but when I took off her shoes, I discovered that they were filled with sewer water and fecal matter.

"The bathrooms at the Superdome ran over," she replied to my dismayed questions. "But we had to use them anyway."

The amount of suffering I witnessed while working at the Reliant Center really opened my eyes. I know that many people looked at those caught in the middle of the superstorm with disdain, because

I watched them desperately inquire for relief.

they hadn't left when they had the chance. But one thing I found out while serving these amazing survivors was that many of them simply couldn't leave. They couldn't leave because they didn't have the resources.

I watched them desperately inquire about relief, standing in long lines for hours on end just for uncertain promises of assistance. They were completely at the mercy of Uncle Sam and the charitable agencies that served them.

That was where the rubber hit the road for me. My passion was finally ignited. I made a decision—a personal vow—to help everyone I could fulfill their dreams of financial independence. I wanted to empower people to be able to "show up" for themselves, their families and their communities in times of great need. With my background and the financial empowerment programs I had already created, I could really help them—I could teach them how to take care of their resources so they were prepared when a rainy day came.

On the drive home from Dallas, my friend and I talked extensively about our experience, the people we had met and the gratitude we felt at being in a position to be a blessing to others.

We talked about Melvin, a man who declared, like so many others, that he would never return to New Orleans, because the apartment we found for him at a senior living community was the nicest place he had ever lived. We reminisced about spending the night at the hospital with Ben, an older gentleman who complained of chest pains just after thanking me for finding him a new pair of shoes.

During the quiet moments of the drive home, I considered what I needed to do next to further the mission of helping young mothers, couples, grandparents and all the others to be able to respond to such situations in safer, more proactive ways. I felt a buzzing, a churning in my spirit, which I knew would lead me to fulfilling this mission that had already become my life focus.

Storms are always part of life, whether they come in the form of medical situations or natural disasters. Being prepared and having money to address an issue before it becomes a tragedy is of the utmost importance. We need to plan for the best, but also for the

> *Storms are always part of life, whether they come in the form of medical situations or natural disasters.*

worst, and strive to put ourselves in a position where we can help not only ourselves, but others, too.

This experience really made me see how being financially sound allows us the opportunity to help others. So many people told us how much they wanted to help, claiming they would have joined us in Houston or other areas when the need was greatest if they could have. For me, having been successfully self-employed for fifteen years provided me not only with the freedom to suddenly be away for ten days, but also the ability to pay the daily expenses for the unexpected extended stay, which included hotel fees, food and even buying more clothes when needed.

Life is not all about money, but very few dreams can be accomplished without it. Though money doesn't deliver wholesale happiness, neither does poverty. Take care of all of your resources and your life will be easier and more enjoyable.

You can do it. You can be wealthy. Being wealthy means different things to different people—whatever it means to you, I want you to know that it's possible for you and that you deserve it.

What's more, building your financial security will not only serve you well in times of trouble, but will help you serve others, too. And, isn't that what life is really about?

Denice Young, widely known as "America's Cash Flow Expert," is the founder and CEO of Denice Young International—a financial success development firm that teaches individuals, entrepreneurs and business owners the G3 Principle—how to financially "get it, grow it and guard it." Denice has helped many Fortune 500 companies, including IBM, HUGHES, Bank of America, Hewlett/Packard, TransAmerica and ARCO, improve their bottom lines by saving millions of dollars.

Denice is also an international speaker and success trainer, as well as a leading innovator in wealth creation, helping individuals and small businesses all over the world to live and operate more successfully. She strives to empower entrepreneurs to make seemingly impossible financial successes possible by teaching and helping individuals implement processes she has personally used, developed and taught. Connect with Denice at www.DeniceYoung.com.

Christine Sherbert

TAKE YOUR TIME BACK

L ying in my hotel bed, still wide awake, I watched the clock
turn minute by minute on the bedside table and thought
about how much family time my job had taken from me over the
years.

It was the year my father retired from his factory job. He had
given most of his life working as a laborer, trading his time for
dollars. Every day he worked in high heat and, by the day's end,
his clothes would be black. He finally was eligible for retirement
and wanted to celebrate with the whole family. He had always
wanted to take a family trip with his children and grandchildren
and arranged to take us all to Disney.

At the time, I was a single mom raising my daughter, Chrissy,
and working paycheck to paycheck as a full-time government
contractor. My on-site supervisor continually harassed me by
putting me on travel orders, keeping me on the road more than
I was at home. I slowly began to realize that I was trading my
time for dollars, like my father, and it was robbing me of the most
precious commodity: time.

I wanted to go to Disney with the family and put in for my
earned vacation time—but it was denied. My entire family was at
Disney and I was on travel orders for the government. As I lay
in bed, growing more and more frustrated, I reflected on the

early years of Chrissy's life. For years I had been a single mom. It was always difficult to find daycare and babysitters, which made holding down a full-time job almost impossible. When Chrissy was still in her infancy, I had started my own small printing business. When the kids were out of school during the summer, she was at the office with me day in and day out.

One summer, we were scheduled to go away on a seashore vacation. It was pre-booked, pre-planned and paid in full. My daughter was so excited that the night before we were due to go, she barely slept.

The next morning I received a call from my only employee. "I'm sorry," she said, "I know you're going on vacation, but I'm sick and I can't make it into the office."

I've taken this away from her. My heart sank, as I thought about my daughter. *I've taken her vacation and her excitement; these are minutes that neither of us will be able to get back.*

What made me most frustrated, as I tossed and turned, unable to get comfortable or drift off to sleep, was that I couldn't break the cycle. *Here I am yet again in a position where someone else is able to steal time from me, time spent away from the people I love, while they create family memories I'll never be able to share.*

I was trading my time for dollars.

I threw off the covers and turned on the TV, hoping that it would tire me out enough so I could sleep. While changing the channels, I came across a late-night infomercial about how people like me could take their time back using real estate as a vehicle to achieve financial freedom. I'd never even considered real estate before, knew nothing about it, but I was frustrated with my job. On the way back from those travel orders, I attended the free seminar advertised in the infomercial. At the event, I met many others seeking a way out of the paycheck to paycheck cycle. I knew I had come to the right place. The speaker told us we could achieve personal and financial success in real estate and business "without money," and my first thought was, *Yeah, right.* I was in debt, had little credit and knew that in order to reclaim my time, I needed to at least replace my job income.

As the speaker continued, sharing knowledge, techniques and statistics with us, I began sitting up straighter in my seat. I started taking notes and writing down questions to ask at the end, my pen almost flying across my notepad in an effort to take as much away with me as I could.

Suddenly, it all seemed possible—I knew others who were successful and made a good living from rental properties and they didn't seem any different from me. They just had the knowledge I didn't have, yet.

Every minute of every day is a minute that can never be recaptured.

Walking out of the seminar, I vowed to myself, *Never again will I let an employer treat me this way, or steal my time. Never again.*

Within months of attending that first seminar and ongoing workshops, applying the techniques and knowledge I'd gained, I acquired several properties and left my job.

I was honored when Wealth Intelligence Academy (WIA) wanted to interview me for their infomercial and feature my projects to show other women this was also an option for them. I had an offer from WIA to become part of their mentor team and went on to mentor Rich Dad Education students. What an opportunity! I could continue to learn, excel in my business and help others all at the same time—I was teaching exactly what I was doing!

The first morning after I left employment, I took my coffee to the front porch. The grass looked a little bit greener, the sky a bit bluer, and I noticed just how much more beautiful everything appeared. There seemed to be a whole new vision in front of me.

My jobs throughout the years had never allowed me to stop and smell the roses. I floated from job to job, using up all of my vacation time and sick days until I had to take unpaid time off when my daughter needed me. My parents babysat for me in the evenings while I worked as a nighttime bartender—between school and work, Chrissy and I hardly even saw each other at times. I thought there was no other way as I needed to pay the bills and provide for my daughter.

Now, I knew differently. Now, I had the time—perhaps not time freedom, but time flexibility. From the outset of slowly making that transition, I've enjoyed the ability to be flexible with my time in order to meet my family's needs. I was with my mother-in-law during her cancer treatments; I have time to visit my grandmother at the geriatric and rehabilitation center, and I've had the ability to

> *It's never about just making money; it's about what the money can provide.*

provide hospice care for my husband's aunt during the last weeks of her life. She was otherwise alone—she had no children and hadn't remarried after her divorce. Her greatest fear was dying alone or with strangers. To be able to provide that care for her was priceless.

The time we have is so precious. To be with those you care about in a time of need, to have the time to create memories with them— that can't be replaced by any dollar amount. We can never go back and recreate time. My daughter is all grown up and I can't give her those childhood memories she should have had; that's something I still regret. Every minute of every day is a minute that can never be recaptured. These minutes have more value to me than anything else. There is a difference between making a living and living your life.

Since 2004, when I began investing in real estate, my motivation has evolved past the personal. It's about showing others that they, too, can have time and financial freedom, that they can venture out and should never give up on their dream. My mentor and now business partner, Bill Walsh, has made me realize there has to be a big enough "why" to drive you; it can't just be a good idea or notion; it has to be something that is meaningful enough to really move you through challenges.

When I speak with clients and mentor students, I ask them, "Why do you want to do this?"

Their first answer is usually, "I need to make money."

But it has to go deeper. "Why do you want to make money?" I ask.

And they answer, "I've got bills to pay and debt to reduce."

Yet we have to go deeper still, until we get to the heart of their hopes and dreams, find the root of their passion, the "why" that drives them. It's never about just making money; it's about what the money can provide.

The time I lost over the years, working full-time, is gone. I was pretty good at making a living, but sacrificed my time and the time of family and friends. The more I succeeded, the less time I spent with them—and years went by before I realized what had happened! My days were spent building my business and I forgot how to have fun—but your life doesn't have to go this way.

As soon as I started making strides to gain the knowledge I'd gone without, before, I started to see results. Get with others who are living the life you dream of and find out their stories. They may just put you on the path where you need to be. You can balance your mind, spirit and business: align with the right mentor, find something you're good at and have a passion for and, if you use resources and put the right systems into place, you can have it all.

When I took my time back, I realized I have so much potential. I have the power to control my destiny. In my office, I now have a clock inscribed, "Time is priceless."

What does financial freedom mean to you? Are you ready to take back your life?

Christine Sherbert is a real estate investor, trainer and mentor, considered an expert in private money transactional engineering; her passion is in helping others to succeed and become profitable. Before investing in real estate, she held a full-time contract position as a networking engineer for the Department of Defense. In 2005, she left her job to pursue real estate investing full-time, and went on to mentor students throughout the United States for national real estate gurus Russ Whitney, Wealth Intelligence Academy and Rich Dad Education. To connect with Christine and start taking your time back, visit www. WealthWithRealEstate.us and www.KeyToBuildWealth.net.

Paula Oleska

THE POWER OF PASSION

E verybody knows that if you want to achieve your goals, you need to have a plan and write it down. I'm sure you've heard: If it's not written down, it's not a goal. You need to give yourself a timeframe and divide your goal into steps; set a schedule and go about achieving your goal step by step. Right?

Not necessarily. As I learned from working with brains, this is the left-brain way of doing things. If you are one of the people who has been trying to succeed that way and didn't accomplish what you set out to do, you may be a right-brain person. Don't despair! There is a way for you to achieve your goals, too. It's called passion. If your passion is powerful enough, it will guide you into achieving it.

I know, because I have done it. I have achieved all of my dreams, including some that I didn't even knew I had! When I set out on my journey, I never wrote a page, never set a timeline.

At that time, people often asked me, "What are your plans?" or "What are you going to do with this?" or "What are you going to do in one year, three year, five years?"

My answer usually was, "I have no idea. The only thing I know is that I have to do *this* right now."

I left my home in then-Communist, repressive Poland to become a dancer. Later on, in New York, I became an opera singer and performed steadily for several years. During that time, I was also studying and practicing new mind-body systems, which eventually led me to develop my own breakthrough program called Brain Upgrade®. I established a successful practice with no previous business background, in a field very few people knew about. I succeeded. Without a written plan.

Don't get me wrong; plans are definitely useful. I have a schedule and plans for the day, the week and several months ahead. But when it came to my bigger goals and visions, I had to follow my path and see where it would take me. That's why I can say: If you are a right-brain person who has trouble planning a step-by-step process, this is your alternative: Cultivate your passion!

Passion works because it uses the parts of your brain that aren't in your head. Through study of the brain and how it functions and what it controls, I learned that the brain is not localized in the head. The brain is a communication network dispersed throughout the body. The brain in the head is a part of that, but it's not the

---

I have achieved all of my dreams.

---

only part. I call the part of the brain that controls the body the behavioral brain; it decides what will be done or accomplished.

Because of that connection, making changes by working through the body is much faster than working through thinking. Thinking is actually a very small and discountable part of our brain function. That may seem strange, but haven't you experienced it already? I'm sure you noticed that you don't think logically when you have the flu or any kind of illness or pain. When you are in distress, you may become forgetful; you may have trouble focusing and thinking. So there you have it: Thinking is a very important part of your brain function, but it is disposable.

Making changes through thinking is very laborious and, in many situations, it doesn't work. Many people I work with say that self-help through working with their minds worked some of the time, but most of the time, not at all. But the machine of self-help still runs in the same direction, which is: You need to change your thinking; you need to control your subconscious mind with your thinking. Visualization, which is a part of this method, is one step beyond thinking, but it is still part of working with your mind: *cognitive approach.*

The alternative is a *kinesthetic approach.* I came to understand, through my work with those parts of the brain that control body and movement, that, in our bodies, we have a vast non-verbal intelligence, which knows much more than our conscious mind. One of the components of that intelligence is our DNA, our genetic blueprint. So our DNA knows where we came from and where we are going and where we are right now. This intelligence will not be fooled by verbal statements that contradict where you are. It says, "Who are you trying to fool? I know better. You can't manipulate me and, unless you give me tools I can work with, we're not going to get anywhere."

If you don't learn to work with your innate intelligence, which has to do with body movement, touch and emotions, the results are going to be only partially effective.

I grew up in a very intellectual environment and I was not in touch with my body. I actually didn't like my body at all. When I read for the first time that the body has an intelligence and you just have to unblock it, I was indignant. *You can't unblock it. My body*

We have a vast non-verbal intelligence.

---

would fall apart if I didn't tell it what do. But my inner intelligence knew better. It led me to learn a system called Touch for Health, which has to do with balancing muscles through a system of reflex touch points.

During an instructor training workshop, I had an incredible experience. I felt as though the top of my head opened and I was no longer learning through my head; I was learning through my body. At that time I didn't know just what learning through my body meant, but I had a complete shift. I was always a good learner, but I focused really hard, which in my current lingo we call over-focus. After the experience at the workshop, I no longer had to focus so hard, because learning happened as if through osmosis.

Over time, many systems developed from Touch for Health; they're now collectively called specialized kinesiology. I decided to use the system called Brain Gym®, which was the only kinesiology that was using movement. Brain Gym's motto is: Movement is the Door to Learning. It reinforced my intuitive understanding that movement and working with the body are keys, not only to learning, but to personal growth.

I developed my own material and made many discoveries to do with various types of movement; I specialized in working with emotions, understanding that our current approach to emotions doesn't work and that there's a better way of working with them. Eventually I formulated a system I call Brain Upgrade® which has

Find your passion and let it guide you.

to do with behavioral and emotional change to help people achieve their goals in a different way.

Some people have a vision for their lives and futures and are too much in the right brain. These people see the big picture of where they want to be, but they don't have the ability to break down that big picture or vision into steps so they can actually go about achieving it. Using my techniques, which have to do with integrating the two parts of the brain, they develop access to their left brain so their sequential thinking kicks in and they can see a path toward achieving their vision. Then they also need to enlist the behavioral brain in the project, so they can actually take action and move toward their vision.

When people run into obstacles in achieving their goals or visions, it's the behavioral brain putting brakes on the process. Behavioral brain doesn't like change, so it will stop you if it perceives the change to be a threat. The mind says, "Oh that? That's such a small thing; it doesn't matter." But the behavioral brain says, "Oh no, this is really dangerous; we can't go there." That obstacle might be as simple as cleaning out a pile of paper, which, on the behavioral level, may serve as a security blanket. You can't argue with your behavioral brain because it controls your muscles. But working with it through kinesthetic methods will dissolve the obstacle so you can move forward.

As I have been telling you, I'm a strong believer in following your passion. But passion alone would have led me astray, because I am interested in many things and I also could not correctly evaluate how long it would take me to accomplish different projects. It took brain integration techniques to help me focus on my priorities and become realistic about timeframes. Now I'm still following my passion, but instead of being a jack-of-all-trades, I am much more organized, selective and I also have fun. Now my mind really helps because instead of dictating how things should be, it helps organize my path. Because now it follows the lead of my emotional brain, passion, and my behavioral brain, action.

Passion follows from the innate intelligence of the entire brain, the communication network in the body, going far beyond the left brain and the right brain. What I want to inspire you with right now is this: You can succeed even if you have no support, low self-esteem and no confidence. I did. I often had to go my own way against powerful disapproval from my family and discouragement from others. I was a beginner with every new endeavor and had to learn tremendous amounts of new things. These five principles allowed me to succeed, even when I had no faith in myself:

- My passion would not let me rest. It gave me a visceral feeling: "this is what we are going to be doing now," even if I didn't know how it would be done. I allowed my passion to guide me.
- I took risks.
- I was open to learning new things.
- I was persistent.
- I organized my brain with kinesthetic techniques.

I'm passing those principles on to you. I want you to believe that you can succeed right now, right from where you are—even if you don't know how, even if you don't have money or support. Get in touch with your gut, find your passion and let it guide you. It will definitely take you places—even if they are not exactly what you had thought. But it *will* be an adventure.

Paula Oleska, MA, has been teaching new ways of developing intelligence for over twenty-five years. She has created a new modality, Brain Upgrade®, which uses movement, touch and emotional exercises to create super brain breakthroughs in every area of life. She has helped over seven thousand individuals achieve breakthroughs in self-esteem, hyper-productivity, super effective communication, creative problem solving and more.

Paula has designed new, proprietary seminars where participants switch on their brain power and discover The Keys to Real Wealth, The Wisdom of Anger, How To Be a People Whisperer and many more. She has been a sought-after speaker at local and international conferences and a bestselling author of three books. She maintains a very busy private consulting practice in New York City. Connect with Paula at www.BrainUpgrade.biz.

Danielle Nistor

DIVINE CONTRACT

On my first night in the arid, sandy hills of Medjugorje, a village in the western region of Bosnia and Herzegovina, I heard a voice whisper softly to me: "Don't be afraid. We are the angels of Mother Mary and we are here to tell you to be ready as your mission will start soon."

You must have imagined that, I thought. Although I had long yearned to go on a sacred pilgrimage to Medjugorje and had come in search of my own purpose, before embarking on the journey I had felt disconnected from my self, my family, the Earth for so long that it did not occur to me the voice was real.

I was born in communist Romania within borders that were closed to the outside world, discouraged from exploring or practicing spiritual and religious beliefs. At that time, one could find very few books on spirituality, most of them Xeroxed copies of old foreign books that were officially forbidden but were distributed freely by book lovers.

In my search for meaning and purpose, I attended church services, prayed devotions at home and attended courses on spirituality and healing.

Even after years of study and practice, something big was still missing from my life. When I discovered the compelling stories of the pilgrims who had reconnected with Divinity and their higher selves through travels to sacred places of divine presence, I decided to make the journey myself.

Medjugorje is truly a magical place and words are too poor to describe it. On June 24, 1981, the first local apparition of the Virgin Mary took place on the "Hill of Apparitions" and ever since the site has become an international place of pilgrimage. The essence of a holy place and the energies of the Divine protector of the place are even more powerful here in its home and they are enhanced by the prayers of all the pilgrims who have traveled to the sacred site. Once here, you step into a different world in which you are amazingly sustained by the wonderful energy of Mother Mary and of the place itself; there is nothing you need anymore—no food or sleep—and a deep sense of peace and love carries you as on a dove's wings.

The night after I heard the voice, I was walking back to my hotel from the evening service. One of the girls in our group was running in the opposite direction, so I stopped her to ask why. "In about thirty minutes, Ivan, one of the visionaries, will receive a message from Mother Mary on top of the 'Hill of Apparitions,'" she said.

I ran fast to the hotel to let others know of the event and then quickly hopped in a cab with a couple of people to go up to the hill.

"We are the angels of Mother Mary."

I had heard many stories of this famous hill where, for a long time, many apparitions of the Virgin took place and many messages from her were given.

When we arrived, the whole area was immersed in darkness, except for a few lanterns carried by pilgrims climbing the hill, shedding light on the pathway for everyone else. When I reached the top, I noticed that, although a sea of people were gathered there, a sacred silence enveloped everyone and everything.

We took a place among the other pilgrims standing and waiting. I could not see the spot where the visionary was standing and I closed my eyes and started praying. Suddenly, I felt a rush of hot and powerful energy enveloping me and running from my head down through my spine. I felt a tingling sensation in my feet. I looked down and saw a silver globe, small as a golf ball, with Mother Mary's figure inside it, standing with her arms open with a white cross behind her. The globe with the Virgin stayed there for a while and then faded into thin air. I was transfixed and marveled at this vision and, to tell you the truth, I was not even fully aware of what I had just seen.

Within a few minutes, I came back to reality and I heard from the people around me the divine message that Ivan had received that day. We went back to our hotel on foot; everyone was talking

We took a place among the other pilgrims.

about what they felt when the message was received. I only had the courage to tell them that I had felt a hot energy. I truly believed that the silver globe was purely my imagination and I did not want to make a fool of myself.

The next morning, Marija, a visionary who was receiving messages regularly from Mother Mary, was going to receive the monthly message that very day, so we went with the whole group to attend the event.

The sky above was a crisp blue on that perfect morning, with a soft breeze and all the birds chirping in the trees and in the bushes. I saw many shiny orbs all around and, all of a sudden, everything became silent and still. I could feel that something special was going to happen.

We entered the Cenacolo garden, where the event was going to take place, and sat down on one of the benches, which were arranged in rows. I sat there with the palms of my hands turned up toward the heavens and all my senses open, willing to absorb and remember everything around me. All of a sudden, I started to receive showers of hot and cold energy, until my body trembled so strongly and out of control that I was afraid I would lose my balance and fall back on the people behind me. I stood up and looked at the sky and I prayed.

We were all quiet waiting for the divine message; my body started to relax and I thought, *How wonderful it would be to receive a message myself.* I cannot find the words to express what I felt when a message poured into my mind: "Dear ones, thank you for gathering here to hear my words. Pray to me and have faith as my Son did when He walked amongst you. You are my children and you are dearly loved. Forgive one another and pray for peace and salvation for the whole world."

I was in awe at what I had just heard when the soft voice continued with these words addressed directly to me: "I ask you, my dear child, to be the messenger of my divine love and share my messages of hope, wisdom and support and my healing energies with all the people. You are to be a channel, a writer, a healer and a teacher; a true divine connector who shall bring words and energies of grace, love and support to the people and your work shall start now. You shall receive messages every day and you shall publish a book of messages in order to share our wisdom, support and advice."

In that profound silence in the garden, I heard the cry of a child and I saw the vision of Mother Mary in front of me for the first time in my life: She was standing on a white puffy cloud as she was lifted to Heaven, waving good-bye to us all with her right arm. Her pure love and perfect beauty, the peace and compassion emanating from her, overwhelmed me so much that I started crying, with sobs coming from the inner core of my being. I cried as I had never cried before in my life, until I was wiped out and collapsed on the bench.

For months after my pilgrimage, I lived in a state of complete grace, joy and inner peace. Everything around me seemed perfect and the world was beautiful, because I saw life through divine lenses. Since then, I have had the privilege of receiving many visions of Mother Mary and messages from her, but that first time and her image on the cloud stayed with me forever, imprinted in my heart and mind.

After Medjugorje, I went on many sacred journeys to other holy places of pilgrimage, such as Lourdes, Altotting, Fatima, Loretto, Compostela and the Holy Land. I shared in the energy of Mother Mary in all these places and she always sent me messages of love and healing. In time, I was blessed with more messages from other beings of light and Ascended Masters as well. By accepting the invitation to become a spiritual messenger and a divine connector, I found it was easy to let go of my own vulnerabilities and become a channel of transformation in other people's lives.

The higher truth and the messages coming from the divine wisdom made me understand and come to terms with my life and for the first time I understood my own story from the perspective

---

Shine your spirit.

---

of my soul: My mission here as a soul messenger of love and hope is to help people heal by connecting them to a higher purpose. My life story, everything that happened to me before that moment of enlightenment, had prepared me for my lifework.

My personal message is: You are precious, you are loved and you are divine. Tend lovingly to your gifts, strive to expand their reach and give yourself permission to be all that you can be.

The divine message for each one of you is: "You are all my children, you are an extension of the divine, you are emissaries of light born to create a new world of love, hope and joy for all. Please ask for guidance and be open to receive the gifts of the spirit in your life. You are never alone. Fill your heart with love and receive our divine blessings right now. Shine your spirit, embracing the planet within your light."

We are always taken by the hand and put onto our true paths in different ways. A recurring dream, a message, an intuition, a hunch that you are supposed to be or do something, is usually felt early on, in childhood; a connection with a great mentor, a teacher, someone who sees something in you and brings out the real you; movies and books that create a strong emotion in you—awakening your inner knowing—these are all ways of connecting you with that moment of truth that is already present in your soul.

We have full divine contracts when we come to earth and we know exactly what we are supposed to do with our lives, how our own divine purpose connects to the divine purpose of others and how it is all connected in a divine net that is designed to transform the planet. Your life's work is to be fully yourself, to understand the intricacies of your story, while accepting the fact that this story serves you, to support your own transformation—so that you can become the person you are supposed to be and to empower you to fulfill your purpose: your divine contract.

Believe in your divine purpose. Follow your true path. Cherish life. Step into your greatness now!

Danielle Nistor is a divine connector, transformational speaker and inspirational writer. Through her work, she empowers people to step into their purpose, connect with the Divine and unfold their spiritual self. Thousands of people around the world have been inspired and empowered by her compassionate guidance and intuitive truth-telling. Working with empathy and passion in her intuitive healing process, Healing in Spirit, Danielle facilitates and has witnessed many miracles and countless healings in her practice. She shares messages of divine love in pilgrimages to sacred places and in spiritual group meditations and workshops in the United States, Canada and Europe.

Danielle holds a BA in international law and she is certified in many healing modalities. Before she began her work as a healer, writer and teacher, she worked as a fashion model. She is the author of Soul Lessons of El Camino: A Miraculous Journey of Visions and Spiritual Messages *and* Understanding Depression: A Spiritual Guide that Brings Hope and Light to the Soul. *Connect with Danielle at www. HealingInSpirit.com.*

Connie K

HEALING HEARTS AND CHANGING HABITS

I shifted the car into reverse and backed out of my driveway. Just for a moment, I thought, *"Is this a wild goose chase? Here I am, taking a journey into the unknown, spending a lot of money to see a hypnotist I haven't met. Will it work? Am I being foolish"*? But then I realized failure was not an option; it *had* to work. I just couldn't go on like this, obsessing about food, constantly dieting and then gaining it all back. I needed help to get my mind off food. During the long drive through Montana's Big Sky Country, I thought about how I had come to this state of mental exhaustion about food.

I remembered that day in junior high when my dentist told me the news. Something was wrong with the mechanics of my mouth structure and my braces weren't fixing the problem. He told me if I didn't correct things immediately, I could have jaw pain and impaired speech later in life. The solution would involve inserting a cage-like contraption, complete with vertical metal bars, into my mouth. Although I would not be able to talk for a while, he said it would be worth it in the long run.

I couldn't imagine not being able to talk. (My parents had always joked that they had named me "Constance" appropriately, as I was "constant"ly talking.) But I had no choice. The procedure had to be done. Insertion of the cage was extremely painful. Not only was I unable to talk, eating was quite difficult.

I remembered hiding in a bathroom stall at school during lunchtime, slurping down a jar of baby food. It was about the only food that would slide between the bars in my mouth. I was so hungry for real food; I dreamed about eating real food. But I was limited to eating soft food or ground up mush. I slowly descended into obsessing about food, all the good things I couldn't have while that cage was in my mouth.

I got through this ordeal the only way I knew how: by having a sense of humor about it. My parents taught me fortitude. Self-pity was never allowed. A mouth full of metal was miserable, but I had to make the best of it. Even though I tried to remain positive, I had some rough days. It is not always easy to laugh it off when other kids make fun of you. I didn't always feel like going to school. I decided to concentrate on my studies; I put my focus and energy on things I could control.

I knew everything was for a reason. I also knew that through adversity, something good would come. I vowed that one day, not only would I speak again, I would have a message to share.

Later on in high school, the cage and braces were finally removed. I could finally eat regular food again. And did I eat! I enjoyed all the delectable delights that had been off-limits for so

I needed help to get my mind off food.

long. I started putting on pounds. I began worrying about my weight, but I couldn't stop eating. Food just tasted so good! This led to the endless pursuit of ways to lose the weight. I tried one diet after another; I fasted. I'd lose some weight but then gain it all back, plus more. The problem became even worse when I became a busy stockbroker. Food became an emotional stress reliever after working long hours.

This battle continued for years. My thoughts were constantly on food. Cravings were perpetual. I gave in to temptation one day and vowed to do better the next. Each failure wounded my self-esteem and weighed heavily on my heart. I knew *what* to eat, but part of me always seemed to sabotage my efforts. Food had turned into an obsession that was ruining my life. I was exhausted and taking an anti-depressant and realized, *I simply cannot live this way anymore.* I had had enough. I decided to consult a hypnotist. I had done a lot of reading and knew hypnosis could help with many issues, especially when a person is ready to change. I was *more* than ready!

Today was the day. I arrived at my appointment hopeful, yet nervous. The hypnotist put me at ease and the session was very relaxing. She gave me the suggestion: Whenever a sugar craving hit, I would remember that it was just a thought and a thought could be changed. She also said I could have sugar if I wanted it— that was mind-blowing. I believe those words were the key to my final success, because I stopped judging food and judging myself for the foods I ate. Sugar was no longer bad or good, right or wrong. It was just food. It was neutral. Once I knew at a subconscious level that food had no power over me, the healing began.

It took time to fully trust the power of my mind to overcome my old habits, but I kept on doing what the hypnotist suggested and it worked! I was amazed at how simple things became. I found myself taking daily walks. It had seemed almost impossible to find time to exercise, but now the time appeared. By listening repeatedly to the audio program the hypnotist had given me, I was able to reprogram my mind on a daily basis. I learned to relax about food and live a normal life eating a variety of foods. I came to understand that it wasn't about being perfect; it was about being in tune with my body. My hypnotist also gave me the suggestion that, when ready, I'd feel better and could stop the medication. She was right. After a short time, I was able to get off the anti-depressant and felt enormously better.

Through the power of my mind, I made peace with food. I released the excess pounds, reached my goal weight and have maintained it for the last twenty years. But, more important: Changing my thought habits about food lifted the heaviness from my heart.

If hypnosis could help me *get off the diet roller coaster, then it could also help others.* I learned all I could about hypnosis and trained to become a certified hypnotist. It became my mission to get hypnosis into the mainstream to help others who were trapped in unhealthy habits. I soon discovered that by using the power of the mind through hypnosis, one could not only change habits, but in the process could also heal relationships and resolve other issues. I knew I had found my message to share.

I noticed I was attracting clients who were carrying heaviness in their hearts. Some had lost family members; some were dealing with divorce or unhealthy relationship issues; some were carrying wounds from the past. People would come to lose weight or stop

---

It took time to fully trust the power of my mind.

---

smoking and, after working with me, discover that they felt lighter, more at peace. They could forgive themselves or others for past hurts. Marriages and family relationships were restored. Heavy hearts turned into joyous, thankful hearts.

I knew I had been given a gift, so I sought out more training to become even more skilled in helping people. I trained in several energy therapy techniques and became a master practitioner of neurolinguistic communication skills. I incorporated all these tools into a system to help clients release not only their habits, but their hurts as well. Word spread, my practice increased and now thousands of clients from across the region flock to my clinic.

People come to me feeling powerless over certain habits. Habits are formed in the subconscious mind, which controls most of our thoughts and actions. A habit and a skill are very similar. Whenever we repeat an action or practice a skill, such as learning to swim, ride a bike, or play the piano, our subconscious mind believes it must be important to us; so it begins to build neural pathways for that repetitive movement. Our body begins to repeat the movement automatically and eventually we don't have to think about it anymore. We just swim, ride the bike, or play tunes.

The subconscious mind does not judge whether a repetitive movement is good or bad; its job is to help us remember it. So the subconscious mind does not know the difference between a good repetitive movement like swimming and a bad repetitive movement like snacking on junk food. Once the habit or skill is established, the mind will make sure we remember how to do it. So feeling powerless over a bad habit does not mean that you are out of control, it only means the mind is doing a good job of reminding you. Using willpower to release a bad habit is usually not enough.

The power of the mind can heal your heart.

Willpower comes from the conscious mind. The subconscious mind will always be more powerful when it comes to habits. So we must learn how to access the subconscious mind where the habit is stored. This is where I come in. I use a process that accesses this part of the mind and allows you to change your mindset. Using the wonderful mind tools that I teach, you can reprogram your mind, release old habits and transform your life. Whether you want to lose weight or manage stress; create even more success in business; or heal relationships or past hurts; you must change your mindset.

If you think, *I just can't do it* or *It's not possible for me,* I encourage you to realize that the mind is way more powerful than we've been led to believe. If you have been unable to accomplish a goal or get over a habit or behavior, it is time to do something different. Believe that you can make transformational changes. Believe change is possible for you.

Many people think they have to gather knowledge from outside of themselves, when all of the answers are truly within. We were all designed with enough skills, talents and abilities to succeed. People get caught up, as I was for a long time, in reading too many self-help books or diet books, searching for the answers. There's nothing wrong with gathering information, but to implement all of it, trust that you already know what to do. Sometimes we can access that inner wisdom on our own and sometimes we need a good mentor or trainer to help us. When it comes to the mind, it is useful to have someone guide us past our own roadblocks.

Anything is possible, but it has to fit within your true purpose. Do not be swayed by the "shoulds": what I should do, what I shouldn't do. Instead, trust your heart and listen to your gut. You can do many things, but which ones have meaning to you? Which ones inspire you to be a better person? Which ones are going to keep you healthy, fit and energized?

The mind is very powerful. You are not as limited as you may think. There is always a way out of any uncomfortable situation if you use the right tools. It may take some time and effort, but everything worthwhile does. However, you must *want* to make a change. No one can do it for you. Being the one who makes the changes means you are the one in charge of your life. So, empower yourself! Take back control!

If you are contemplating making changes and the same words that began my journey are echoing in your mind—Will it work? Am I being foolish?—my message is for you. No matter how difficult your circumstances, no matter what happened in your past, you can use the power of your mind to overcome the issues and habits holding you down.

Whether it was a cage in the mouth, a critical parent, the loss of a loved one, bullying or divorce that weighed you down, the power of the mind can heal your heart and put you on the road to authentic success. If you need help, reach for it. I am here. It is worth the journey.

Connie K (Connie Kvilhaug), the "MindSet Mentor," is a neurolinguistics communications speaker, trainer and consultant and the founder and CEO of Billings Hypnosis and the Montana School of Hypnosis. She is a certified instructor of neurolinguistics and hypnosis, training people to break through their limitations and experience transformational changes using the untapped power of their minds. Connie combines the power of these mindset shifts with the power of the heart, creating a strong emotional connection to a successful outcome. She has been asked to speak to several businesses, government groups and organizations across the region and the country. Her message is one of empowerment and inspiration.

Connie trains individuals and groups to support the positive changes they desire, including topics such as: "Empower Your Mind to Win"; "Managing Stress in the Workplace"; "Improving Relationships"; "Golf is a Mind Game"; "How to Get Rapport with Customers and Coworkers" and topics tailored to specific needs. She is available for speaking and consultations with corporations and organizations that want to reduce healthcare costs by helping employees stop smoking, lose weight and manage stress. Connie trains employers and employees in how to improve organizational health and increase communication skills.

Connie has created the Mindset Mastery System *and* Choose the Path to Freedom—Stop Smoking *audio programs and is writing a book on using self-hypnosis for weight loss to be released in 2014. Connect with Connie at www.conniek111.com.*

Juliette M. Willoughby, Esq.

Battling toward Balance

My doctor sat down beside my hospital bed where I was recovering from surgery. She said, "I'm concerned for you, Juliette, because you don't understand pain. The surgeon found fresh blood, which means a fresh rupture. Other people with such a rupture would have been in the emergency room, crying for the doctor to do something about the pain. But you went to court. You need to reeducate yourself about pain and take care of those signals, because next time, who knows what could happen."

I retorted, "I've been in pain for nearly thirty years. If I didn't ignore it, I'd never do anything or go anywhere. And I had to be in court—I had a case and clients depending on me."

She didn't push the issue; she knew me well enough to understand that I don't take kindly to pushing.

I had collapsed in the conference room at the courthouse. One of the judges, who had been a nurse, came flying. Quickly, the paramedics were summoned, and I was whisked to the hospital. I'd been suffering for many years, but the doctors had been unable to make a diagnosis for twenty, and then for ten years told me all they could do was prescribe more and stronger pain medication. Even now, in this crisis, it took them almost two weeks to make a diagnosis. As it turned out, only 125 cases like mine had ever been reported. I had had endometriosis since I was twelve, and now, endometrial cells had migrated to the pleural cavity around my lungs and caused serious bleeding.

The two weeks I spent in the hospital were filled with pain, confusion and work. I was afraid to move because of the agony that would ensue from the chest tube. Yet I still kept working. They put me in a private room, so I could continue to prepare for an upcoming trial.

Four months later, I was finally going to have what would be the cure for my unique situation. I was scheduled to be in the hospital for three days; I was in for nine. I remember a former student, who spent every night in my room, rushing out into the hallway calling to the nurses, "You've got to give her something for the pain."

I had collapsed in the conference room.

I felt so vulnerable, with a tube down my throat, unable to speak or eat. And I remember that my father came to see me three times. He hated hospitals and had never visited me in a hospital before. My mother, who had always been my rock, started to show cracks. That's how I knew I was in trouble.

I was terrified that I wouldn't make it out of the hospital. I thought, *I'll never have a chance to accomplish all the things I should have because I'm going to die.*

I had been teaching social work at Atlantic Union College in Massachusetts, in the same department as my mother. When that department closed, we both lost our jobs. Now, I'd had a hysterectomy and would never have children. I had lost so much; I knew I had to find myself, or I would die.

When I was teaching, I always spent the first three weeks on self-development. The semester the department was closed, I had intended to use Jack Canfield's book *The Success Principles*. Leafing through it, I noticed that he offered free one-day seminars in various places around the country. I loved his books and took the opportunity to see and hear the man in person. I loved what he had to say and later went to Breakthrough to Success in Arizona.

I learned more and more about myself, battling my own fears and limitations. I realized that pain is a signal of trouble and that "working through it" should not be an option. After about a year and a half, I became a certified coach. And then, the battle intensified. My work as a lawyer is with indigent people who really need my services. I advocate for them in child protection cases, helping them get the services they require and representing them in court. But I wanted to coach lawyers.

Lawyers have the fourth highest suicide rate, behind dentists, pharmacists and physicians; medical professionals have more access to deadly drugs. Lawyers are 3.6 times more likely to suffer from depression than the general population and many struggle with alcohol and drug addictions.

I believe that lawyers are the "garbage dump of society." We see and hear all society's ills but can't talk about them. Even when the client is dead, we must keep our clients' confidentiality. When I taught social work, I taught students how to decompress. Social

---

I was in the perfect spot to help.

---

workers and therapists always have their own social workers and therapists, because they take in so much negative energy and know what harm it can do to them. But lawyers are not taught how to decompress. I was in the perfect spot to help.

I have a certificate for coaching; I have a master's in social work and I'm a lawyer. Why not take care of my people? And I was right for the job, because I was just learning how to take care of my body. Lawyers think they are untouchable, but we need care, respect and someone to know what we do and carry on a daily basis.

But the thought of abandoning my indigent clients filled me with debilitating, immobilizing guilt. During my journey of self-discovery, I met wonderful people, life-long friends. I could talk to them about my battle with guilt. Eventually it became clear that if I helped other lawyers, that would also help non-lawyers, including my indigent clients. But, if I just helped my indigent clients, who would help the lawyers? When they demonstrate how to use an air mask, flight attendants tell passengers, "Get your own mask on first, even before you try to help your children. You can't help anyone if you can't breathe."

I could help lawyers, and other people who are subsumed in their work, such as writers and entrepreneurs and moms, save themselves, so that they could then help others. Sometimes saving

---

Balance is a marathon.

---

yourself is the single best contribution you can make. And balance is the method by which we save ourselves.

Paradoxically, to begin your battle toward balance you must first surrender. You must surrender the idea that you can be all things to all people at all times. Otherwise, you will keep going at a hundred miles an hour and neither your body nor your mind can withstand that.

Secondly, get truly in touch with your core values—not general values, core values. When you get in touch with your core values, other things slough off and disappear, because they are not intrinsically important to you. You will start to focus on those pieces that are part of your core values; they will take up more and more room, so there won't be room for the pieces that are not truly part of who you are.

Thirdly, develop your road map so that, when you start to deviate (we all do) and go down a path where you get sucked in again and start to get lost, you can use that road map to get back to your core. Without a map, we flounder trying to get back on track. With a map, we can just follow it—not create something new.

I have determined what success means for me and then battled to reach it. When you are young, people tell you what success means. And as you climb the ladder of what success means to them, you may find that you've placed your ladder against the wrong building—that your success is something entirely different. Go ahead and start over, but take with you those rungs of the ladder, those skills, which can help you climb the next building. Renegotiate and redistribute your skills into your new or different venture. Each skill is unique to you. You may be a doctor, a lawyer, an entrepreneur, a parent—nobody does it the way you do and you can always move your ladder to reach success as you define it.

In the hospital, I was "full-speed ahead" even though I couldn't get out of bed. Learning balance has been a battle. One great battle and victory was at Warrior Camp, a personal development camp offered through Peak Potentials. Asking for help, being vulnerable and saying I can't do this or that has never been my strong suit. I was always the one who could conquer anything physical. If it needs to be moved or carried, just ask Juliette. But, in two of the events, I wasn't the strong person who could muscle through anything. I had to admit vulnerability. I had to ask for help. It was a real learning experience.

In that setting and with those people, asking for help wasn't seen as a weakness, vulnerability was seen as a strength. Only through vulnerability could I truly be seen and truly see myself. This was the only way that I could see who I was and all that I could be. Giving myself permission to be vulnerable also helps me help others give themselves permission to find all the possibilities life holds for them.

Now that I don't have to carry the weight of the world, I find that I'm more able to hear my clients' stories and more able to hear my own story. I can more easily forgive myself for my own foibles and weaknesses. I'm more in touch with the time that has passed and what I want life to be like in the present and in the future. I realize that I am a work in progress and that's okay, because balance is a marathon, not a sprint, and I'm willing to battle to achieve my own success.

Today, I am sure of my true calling and thankful for my near-death experience, as it led me to a new passion for life, as well as an even greater passion for helping my fellow lawyers.

Juliette Willoughby, Esq., MSW, JD, earned her bachelor's degree in social work from Atlantic Union College, her master's in social work from the Boston University School of Social Work and her doctorate in jurisprudence from the Massachusetts School of Law. Her practice in South Lancaster focuses on the integration of social work and the law. Juliette taught social work at Atlantic Union College; she was personnel manager for Stafflink and also worked for Tri-Valley Elder Services, St. Vincent's Hospital, the Massachusetts Department of Mental Health and the R. F. Kennedy Action Corps Children's Center. Certified through Dream University, Juliette is a professional coach, helping people achieve balance between work and life. Connect with Juliette at www. LawyersLivingABalancedLife.com.

Teriann Matheson

Eyes Wide Open

What can be more thrilling than opening your own business, living your dream, bringing your very own idea to the public marketplace, being your own boss? When your business is successful, it provides financial freedom and a wonderful lifestyle for you and your family.

Beyond that, it allows you to hire staff, who can then provide for themselves and their families; you can even fund training to advance their skills. And further still, it lets you share your earnings with your community—maybe sponsoring a sports team, or giving a scholarship to a high school graduate, or donating your product to a local fundraiser, or simply supporting local shopkeepers with your purchasing power.

As small businesses are the cornerstone of our economy, the success of a small business has a ripple effect from the owner out into the community as a whole. And so does the failure of a small business. Sadly, over eighty percent of small businesses fail. Many of those failures are preventable, if entrepreneurs keep their eyes open and get educated before they begin. They can be successful from day one, if they start the right way.

I never thought about being a business owner while I was growing up. A year as an exchange student in California created a longing to see all the amazing things the world had to offer and I decided to become a travel agent. While at travel college, I worked in a bakery to pay my way through school. I graduated and launched into the travel industry full-time. But I had just bought a house and was struggling to make ends meet; I wasn't making it sending everyone else on vacation. My boss at the bakery offered me full-time work and I left the travel industry to run a bakery.

I gradually learned how to run all aspects of the business and found I enjoyed the challenges. When the opportunity to buy my own bakery came, I jumped at it. It was a tremendous learning experience, having my own money invested and my name on the line. I enjoyed large profits, with lots of discretionary cash; I gained a reputation for being a crack business operator. Two and a half years later, I sold it. I was thirty years old and had two hundred thousand dollars in cash!

It was more money than I had ever seen in my life. Doing anything productive and long-term with the money was not really on my radar; it was playtime! I took a year off, renovated my house, bought a big present for my brother's wedding and splurged on holidays.

My ego was enormous and my confidence was sky high. A year later, I decided to buy a struggling business. I thought, *I can turn it around and make a huge sum of money again. This is easy!* Famous last words! My parents decided to invest, as I'd had such a great return before. I thought, "I can make you some money. I've got the Midas touch!"

My ego took over and I closed my eyes to warning signs. I didn't look at the numbers properly. The business was seasonal, so cash flow was an issue. My rent was huge—twice normal—and I wasn't breaking even, but I went ahead and bought the business anyway. As my business struggled, I was forced to lay off staff, work six or seven days a week and pay myself just two hundred and fifty dollars a week—it was all the business could afford. I couldn't sponsor any of the events the business had sponsored before, as the business couldn't afford it. My huge lump sum of cash was gone. I was about to go bankrupt and take my parents with me.

It was the most stressful, gut-wrenching, soul-destroying experience I have ever been through. I spent many a sleepless night trying to work out how I was going to pay the huge rent every month. Every single thing I tried to turn the business around failed to work. At two in the morning on one of those sleepless nights I thought, *I was smart to take out life insurance for the business loan for one hundred and fifty thousand dollars. It will pay back the loan and leave enough for my funeral. I've had it longer than thirteen months, so it will pay in the event of suicide. I can make this mess go away if I kill myself.*

I lay there on the couch with my dogs and planned it all out. I thought about the instructions I would leave telling my husband and parents to use the insurance money to pay my debts, so that they wouldn't lose everything. I honestly thought suicide was the only way I could get all of us out of the mess I had made. I was so

---

I enjoyed large profits.

---

exhausted that I was emotionless, except for a feeling of relief that I was finally going to be able to do something that would work, after all the things I had tried that failed to change anything. I was at peace with the decision I had made. I truly felt it was the only way forward.

About two hours later, as I was planning the details of how I was going to do it, a voice inside my head told me that I was copping out. It was my own voice, telling me that killing myself would leave a bigger mess. It told me that to put the burden of my suicide on my family was unfair and selfish. I knew in my heart of hearts that this was true. I pictured my mum crying when someone told her that I had taken my own life, "But don't worry, her life insurance will take care of the debt." Suicide might have taken care of this mess for me, but it would only begin for them. I just couldn't do that.

I told myself to get a grip, grow up, fix things and not take the easy way out. And I reached all the way down into my being and

I did just that. I pushed harder to negotiate a new sublease, which decreased my overhead. I took on training roles for my franchisor, which gave me some help and also some extra money. I worked hard to grow the business. Two years later, I sold it for fifty-five thousand dollars more than I had paid for it. The best day ever was when I gave my parents their money back, plus an extra twenty thousand. I was proud, relieved and absolutely, down to the bone, exhausted.

Now I try, with my utmost, to assess the profitability of any business that I get involved in. I look at the numbers, I look at the area and the possibility to grow and get new customers; I look at

Killing myself would leave a bigger mess.

the long-term viability of the business. I look at the downsides and I plan for them. I will never get myself in a mess like that again.

Our new business employs both my husband and me, and supports our three children. We have fifteen employees—five full-time and ten part-time. Most of the part-time staff are paying their way through school, just as I did. We have invested some of our profit in rental properties, which provide housing for thirteen people.

Our bakery gives away more than three hundred and fifty thousand dollars' worth of bread each year to places like the Salvation Army, recovery houses and church groups, which then distribute it to needy people. We also give donations and sponsorships to schools and sports clubs on a monthly basis.

My husband Leigh and I talk about the business prosperity cycle, which includes the profits that support our family and staff; the money we invest in training staff to upgrade skills; the investments we make in real estate that house some of our neighbors; and our outreach into the wider community. Contrast that with my struggling business that was such a drain on me and on my family members, on the employees I had to lay off and, had I defaulted on my debts, on other businesses as well. A failed business contracts and costs time and energy for its owner and, through a ripple effect, for many, many others.

We train new franchisees and tell them to look at all aspects of how owing a business will affect them. Before leaping in to a business, you need to consider your family time, because owning a business means hard work and long hours. Examine your expectations for the business and its profitability—it will take longer—maybe much longer—than you think to see big profits. Think about what will happen if success doesn't eventuate. Have a plan to get out as well as the plan to expand or grow.

Enjoy the thrill of starting your business, but go into it with your eyes wide open. Be smart and get information that will help you make great choices. Find the right people to have on your team, such as an accountant, a lawyer, a bookkeeper; ask them the right questions. Talk to your family about what owning a business will

Success in business has a ripple effect.

be like and make sure that they are on board and that everyone's expectations are realistic. Look at the numbers and plan for the worst. Have a cash reserve to carry you through rough times. And go into your business planning for the business prosperity cycle and how you can contribute.

If you don't do what you're born to do, if you decide you're not going to pursue this dream or open this business because it is too scary, you're not just letting yourself down. You're cheating all the other people who would benefit from it. And if you're not successful at it, then all those people you might have affected have lost out because you've let your fear, your lack of preparation or whatever, stop you from doing what you're truly meant to do. Being a business owner is wonderful and I wouldn't do anything else, but only if one is smart and knowledgeable.

When you set up your business plan, or plan for the next year, consider the business prosperity cycle. Open your eyes wide to the many people your business affects. How many more people can you include? Your impact comes from what your decisions can do for people. And considering other people keeps you from taking the easy way out; it motivates and feeds back to you in a cycle of success.

True business owners are successful before they even begin, because they get help. They are certain of their knowledge and abilities, and they ask for help with things that are new and unknown.

Find the right people to help you, to shorten your learning curve and to share their experience with you. My mission is to make sure that no one has to go through what I went through and to help create successful businesses, which give back.

Success in business has a ripple effect—how will your business make an impact on the world?

Teriann Matheson holds certificates in small business franchising and frontline management, and has a diploma in travel. She owned a bakery franchise in Australia for two and a half years, and achieved the highest sales volume for one week in the entire seven hundred-store network. She also turned around a Boost Juice Bar franchise and sold it at a profit. She has trained several master franchisees for Boost Juice Bars, who have then opened the franchise business in England, Singapore, Hong Kong, Indonesia and Malaysia. Teriann and her husband, Leigh, own a Cobs Bread bakery and Success Business Solutions and have written The Top 7 Solutions to New Business Owner Challenges *and developed The Business Buying Blueprint, a step-by-step system on how to buy the right business with confidence. Connect with Teriann at www.SuccessBusinessSolutions.com.*

Dr. Sarah Arnold

HIDDEN IN PLAIN SIGHT

"Why are the cops at my front door?" I thought, as I looked out my window to see why my dogs were barking. The officers saw me looking out, so I had to answer the door. I didn't recall breaking any laws, but having the police at your front door usually isn't good news, so I felt uneasy.

As I invited them in, they asked if I knew the whereabouts of my friend Dawn, because she was missing from the hospital. Dawn, a Navy nurse, and I, a Navy doctor at the time, worked together at a previous duty station. We went our separate ways, as we all do in the Navy after a tour is over. I was in a residency program and she was stationed at another clinic.

So, I was surprised to see her at the hospital where I was working. A couple of days before the police showed up on my doorstep, I had lunch with Dawn in the food court at the hospital. That was the last time I saw her. I still had the receipt from Taco Bell—it was my treat.

One of the officers said, "You may have been the last person who remembers seeing her, because shortly after your lunch, she was reported missing from the hospital. We were given your name because she has to sign in and out from the ward and tell the staff who is with her." The officers left me a business card with instructions to call if I saw or heard from her.

I tried to remember earlier conversations to figure out where she could be. I remembered something strange she said a few weeks before when she was at my promotion ceremony. She congratulated me and said, "It's been a pleasure knowing you and working with you." That's when I had suggested we meet for lunch the following week. Now I frantically called her cell phone number and left a message to call me immediately. I was afraid she was in trouble.

Dawn wouldn't tell me why she was in the hospital, so I thought something must have happened at her new duty station. All I knew about her medical history was that she had had a traumatic brain injury, from a car accident I think. When we worked together, she did okay. She was a hard worker and lived by herself while her husband and children lived about three hours away.

Dawn didn't like her job, but neither did most of us. We were always understaffed because of deployments or nervous about being taken out of our clinic to deploy. The only shore duty was for training programs such as the one I was in. Dawn always seemed lonely and kept to herself. She was also very thin; I hardly saw her eat. In fact, the strange thing about having lunch with her that day was that she actually ate her entire meal in front of me.

The next couple of days after meeting with the police officers were uneventful. I was really busy with my training program and still hadn't heard from Dawn. Then, I checked my email. My heart sank as I read an email from a mutual friend saying Dawn was found hanging from a tree in a park near the hospital. My mind immediately went back to the words from the police officer—"You may have been the last person who remembers seeing her"—words I haven't forgotten. After all, I am a primary care physician. Dawn was my friend and colleague; she never seemed happy, but must have been profoundly depressed, and I missed it—and I live with that every day.

Less than a year later, I was deployed in Iraq for the second time and received a very upsetting email from my friend Larry, an Air Force physician who had just finished the residency program with me months before. A mutual friend of ours, Joel, also an Air

Force physician, had driven to a remote location and shot himself in the head. He was found dead by local police the following day. *Not again,* I thought.

That was such a terrible year—two of my friends died by suicide and I was deployed in Iraq. I had to miss my younger brother's wedding because of that deployment, which happened around the time of the bad news of Joel's death. When I was in Iraq, my feelings

> ## I was afraid she was in trouble.

were on edge anyway, so that bad news and my homesickness and guilt from not being at my brother's wedding just made things worse.

For some reason, feelings are just stronger overseas, and then more bad memories and feelings would come up and the nightmares would come back. Over and over again in my dreams, I'd see Dawn hanging from some tree or Joel slumped over in his car with a bullet in his head. The words from the police would stick in my head and I'd hear them louder and louder. More memories and nightmares from previous deployments haunted me as well. Meanwhile, my family was celebrating my brother's wedding and another Thanksgiving and Christmas without me.

While I was able to call friends and family, I always had to be careful what I said and how I said things, because the last thing I wanted was having anyone worry about me. I thought about talking to the chaplain or mental health unit on base, but I just felt uncomfortable. I was a senior officer and it's really awkward to be seen needing that kind of help.

When I got home, I decided to seek help from a civilian therapist on my own dime so I could be completely anonymous. She used several different newer modalities of treatment and, in a couple of months, I started to feel calmer and my nightmares disappeared, but I was still feeling really stressed out and wondered if this was the best I was going to get. I was sleeping better, but still didn't feel good.

One day, I was running late to my appointment, so I didn't have time to change out of my uniform. While I was sitting in the waiting room, an older gentleman recognized my desert utiities. He timidly introduced himself as a Vietnam veteran.

Tears streamed down his face as he said, "I wish I was like you and got what I needed a lot sooner; so much of my life has gone by; so much suffering that didn't need to happen; so many people I

The nightmares would come back.

hurt without realizing it. Thank you so much for your service and never be ashamed for needing help sometimes. Life is so short and far too precious to waste another day suffering when there is help to be had. It seems really bad now, but stick with the therapy, it really will get better."

I thanked him; we both just sat there and cried. I hugged him and asked where he served. We exchanged a few stories, as veterans do, and started laughing, as our stories are similar and timeless— history repeats itself. The receptionist came out and apologized; telling me that my therapist had gone home sick and was unable to see me that day and that she had been trying to call me for the last hour. I hadn't realized so much time had gone by.

"That's okay," I said. "We had our own therapy session right here." The Vietnam vet and I shook hands and parted ways. I was thinking of stopping therapy until I met him. He encouraged me to stick with it and, from then on, I made faster progress.

We often assume that increasing suicide rates in the military have to do with combat tours. But neither of my friends had served in combat. Many of us have experienced mental traumas; personal suffering is a universal human experience. We must never forget, however, that the resilience of the human spirit is also universal. Something kept that Vietnam veteran from killing himself and his experiences and words of encouragement helped me persist with therapy through some bad times. Over the last few years in my own journey of personal development, I've learned that the more

I grow myself, the more resilient I become when dealing with the many challenges in life.

As I reflect on my many tours of duty in the Navy, including my two combat tours in Iraq, on all those deaths I couldn't prevent no matter how hard I tried, the suicides are always the most difficult. As suicides in the military continue to gain media attention, we must remember the friends and family left behind. While suicide prevention programs are necessary, it's important to realize that sometimes the messages become overwhelming to people who lost a friend or loved one to suicide. Messages like, "all suicides are

The universal resilience of the human spirit is stronger than human suffering,

preventable," can leave people feeling guilty and ashamed, which is no consolation after a tragic death. It's just not enough to recognize the circumstances of a potential suicide; we must also be sensitive to the needs of those who lost friends and loved ones.

I wanted to share my story to draw attention to military suicides and yet I also recognize that we can all have stresses, sadness and, yes, sometimes even feelings of anxiety and despair that we hide from others. Working toward our own definition of success, it is easy to become overwhelmed. Reaching for a big goal or dream often requires facing high-pressure situations, pushing past what is comfortable, facing our fears and balancing work, family and other pursuits. Many of us forget about self-care.

Many of us also forget about spirit. It's easy to do when juggling so many obligations. In my experience, "spirit" is a part of me that I have relied on my whole life. It is my inner self, my intuition, or my higher self. In order for me to realize any dream of being "successful," this spirit is intimately involved. If I don't know this, or define this for myself, I don't see how I can be successful.

The universal resilience of the human spirit is stronger than human suffering, but it needs to be fed and nurtured through personal development. The ability to better face daily challenges, to grow beyond obstacles and live the life you envision exists in everyone. It's a process that happens over time when you consciously invest in your own personal development. Take responsibility for your own growth. And if you are experiencing emotional pain that seems too much to bear, or wonder if you may need help dealing with the stresses of life, don't keep it to yourself. Reach out. Ask for help. No matter how sure you may feel that the opposite is true, you are not alone.

Dr. Sarah Arnold is currently a family physician and officer in the United States Public Health Service working for the Department of Defense at the Deployment Health Clinical Center as the Primary Care Proponent for the Patient-Centered Medical Home-Behavioral Health program. Dr. Arnold graduated from Hahnemann University School of Medicine in 1995 and completed a family medicine residency at Naval Hospital Camp Pendleton in 2001 and a preventive medicine residency at the Uniformed Services University of the Health Sciences in 2008. She was a Navy physician for fourteen years, during which she has held several leadership positions in operational medicine and deployed several times, including two tours in Iraq. Her last position in the Navy was acting surgeon, 1st Marine Expeditionary Force, Camp Pendleton, California, where she became intimately involved with combat stress and resilience. She now resides in Gaithersburg, Maryland with her two dogs, Linus and Lucy. Connect with Dr. Arnold at www.BetterHealthStartsTodaycom.

Sarah's story is an expression of her own opinions and experiences and is not representative of the Department of Defense, US Navy, US Public Health Service, or any government agency. Names changed to protect privacy.

National Suicide Prevention Lifeline/Veteran's Crisis Line: 1-800-273-TALK (8255)

Hopeline: 1-800-442-HOPE (4673)

Claude Vigneault

ARE YOU OUT OF BALANCE?

"The doctor wants to see all of us," my older brother told me. "It's about Dad." For almost eighteen months, my father had been experiencing pain and weakness and, though he knew something was off, he was the kind of man who hates to visit doctors. The day I received my brother's call, the family gathered together around my father's hospital bed and the doctor told us, "I'm afraid it's cancer—and it's terminal."

I'd always been afraid of death and could not imagine losing a parent. "There are so many things I would like to tell you," Dad told my sister-in-law and, during the weeks that followed, I hoped the day would finally come that my father would tell me he loved me and was proud of me. But at the end, all he left behind him was a teardrop on each cheek, no passing words of comfort, and I didn't know what any of it meant. All I could think, caught between the pain of losing a loved one and relief that his suffering had ended, was, *How do I want to be remembered after I die? When I'm on my deathbed, I don't want to have any regrets.*

It was my first wake-up call and, not even three months later, I got my second. Two words were all it took for the life I knew to come crashing down around my ears. Two words that shook me to my core and left me completely devastated. "It's over." I'd just come home after another long day of work to find my wife sitting on the couch in the living room, tears running down her face as she looked up at me and told me that she was leaving me.

To say that I was surprised is an understatement. The news completely blindsided me, knocking me off-kilter and leaving me with only the question, "Why?" Until that time, on the whole, everything had seemed good. Over the past few months, I'd noticed that she was not the same and that there was a disconnect between us, but I'd thought, *That happens in every marriage, right?* As I tried to get to sleep the first night she left, tossing and turning in a bed that felt far too big, it was as though everything I had learned when I was a kid was coming back to slap me in the face.

My parents had always had very little money, struggling most months to pay the bills and, more often than not, I would go to school ashamed of having to wear my older brother's hand-me-down pants and shirts. My father was usually working at least two jobs, if not three, to make sure we had food on our plates and I grew up heartbroken that, even though my parents showed love in their own way, nothing ever seemed to be good enough.

I related the fact that I didn't feel loved "properly" to the fact that my father was always away because we needed the money—therefore, I thought, *If I make a lot of money, I'll be happy. I'll be*

I'd always been afraid of death and could not imagine losing a parent.

---

able to buy a lot of stuff; the things my family and I need will never be an issue and I'll be loved.

As I approached adulthood, I was utterly focused on making sure I had no debts and on keeping the promise I had made myself: *I will not just work to live; I will be financially free.* I worked a few jobs to make extra money, but around 1980 it became clear to me that information technology was the future and that was where I directed all of my energy.

Before long I realized that I could make a lot more money if I gave in to my entrepreneurial side and opened a business of my own. But I'd always suffered from a distinct lack of self-confidence, my father's voice always whispering in my ear, "Find a safe job, work hard and you'll be fine."

It was a daily battle, fighting against that fear, but I had to go through that fear in order to be successful.

Constantly driven by making money and finding all possible ways to be loved by people, I invested long hours in growing a business to make it profitable. Most weeks I worked between seventy and eighty hours, rarely taking days off. *A lot of money will bring me love and keep people around me happy,* which was not exactly true. At the age of forty, I was a millionaire after selling my IT company to one of the biggest consulting firms in North

---

I needed to balance my energy.

America; but then I came home to my wife's tear-stained face and those two words that shattered me.

I began to question everything I thought I knew. *Where have I been going so wrong?* I asked myself on a near daily basis, going through the motions of working long hours and coming home to an empty house. *I'm really successful in my business—heck, I became a millionaire! Now I'm on my own with the cash and that's not the way it should be.*

After a few months of feeling like this, my stress levels were so high and my eating habits were so erratic that my body started to send me signs it was time to either slow down or recalibrate my energy. I started working out and, though it was a good way to relieve my stress, it certainly didn't help with the tiredness. One night I finally realized, *I'm worth more than this. I can get control of my life back, but I need to take action and really make a change.*

I believed I could do more. I could use all of these negative emotions as a positive aspect in my life, because I knew I could be better than them—I had been before! Knowing I couldn't really do it with my own mindset clouding any progress I might make, I started trying to think outside the box, reading lots of spiritual books and attending personal growth seminars, which opened my mind not only to the universe but also to the way in which I was expending myself.

Since I was in my forties, it wasn't just the stress that was having an effect on me—it was the energy I was still putting into business ventures such as my IT consulting and real estate and online investments. *I should really reevaluate the way my energy goes, because, if I'm only investing my energy in my business, at some point it will also negatively impact all other areas of my life.*

I came to the conclusion that I needed to balance my energy to make sure I could still do well with my business, but at the same time, if I had a great and positive energy, I'd be open to reevaluating my life priorities. I started really trying to change the way I was eating, sleeping and exercising and found that not only did I have more and more energy, I was also more open to positive signs from the universe.

In the end, it came down to a piece of paper. "Okay, here we go," I said aloud as I sat at my desk one night, having finally decided to try to organize my life. I wanted to get everything written down, so that I could really start to reevaluate what I wanted out of my life and what I needed to do in order to achieve it. *Where do I want to be in ten or fifteen years from now? What is my real life mission on Earth?*

Doing it by myself was complicated, to say the least. I had a lot of good ideas and I knew where I wanted to go, but when I started writing things down—especially the short-term things—I still wasn't sure what to tackle first. What surprised me was that, for once, I wasn't fully organized. In my career, I'd always been the one leading projects, so of course I'd figured, *I can do the same with my life!*

Trying to be organized and listing all of these tasks that were related to each other, more like a mind map than a list, was daunting. But then I reminded myself of a practice I'd employed in my project management of not only having one end goal in mind, but of also having miniature milestones to celebrate.

"We shouldn't just evaluate success at the end," I used to tell my teams and my clients. "We should celebrate that we're successful when we achieve the milestones."

When you're facing tough situations, it's hard to determine that you've had any success, especially small successes—but those are what keep you going.

I started to realize that money was not the only issue—I needed to find the answer to a question I'd been asking myself: *What is my problem with love?* Until I was about forty, I thought money was the most critical thing in my life—but what was missing was being able to love the people in my life properly. I wasn't receiving love properly, nor was I giving love properly. I started with myself,

I now see life in terms of three words: "Everything is possible."

thinking that if I learned how to receive love properly, then I would attract different people, those who knew how to do the same.

Two and a half years after the challenges that changed everything and gave me the push I needed to become the man I am today, I met my current wife—we've been together almost a decade now. I would not have attracted my wife had my priorities not shifted. My priorities have shifted so much that, if I have a new opportunity to invest time and/or money in something, I share it with my family—I want to involve them so they learn how to manage their lives and priorities well.

Before, I only ever considered my career a top priority in my life and that was the root cause of my problems. I keep evaluating all of these interconnected aspects of my life because they affect one another in turn. I still work hard for my financial freedom, but it is now essential in my life to have a balanced, intimate relationship, balanced nutrition and regular workouts and a fulfilling spiritual life.

It's now a priority to make the right choices, properly evaluating their impacts on all major aspects of my life. When you start to better manage your priorities between business and personal, you start to enjoy life.

Take out a piece of paper and start to make your own list. Look at your relationships, nutrition and fitness, spirituality and finance. Where do you stand today? How would you evaluate your situation today? In your dreams, how would you envision your ideal life in each component? In this exercise you start to become the head coach of your own life, looking at areas that need improvement and taking action to realize the dream of success in all areas.

All my life, I viewed success only as being financially free. The way I measure success now is being fully happy with what I'm doing, in all aspects of my life. Being financially free is a form of success; it is one piece of the puzzle, but true success is also being happy in your relationship or marriage, having great relationships with family and friends, feeling healthy in your body and having the energy to feel as though you're unstoppable.

Bad things will happen in your life, but this shouldn't be an excuse to fail to go on, because you will only end up hurting yourself and wasting your precious time. As a certified professional business coach and life coach, a certified yoga teacher and a father for the fourth time at the age of forty-seven, I no longer worry about two words having the power to shatter my world. Instead, I now see life in terms of three words: "Everything is possible."

Claude Vigneault was born in Canada and now shares his time between the United States, Canada and Europe. After finding fortune in the IT industry, he now helps his clients determine how to get clarity on priorities, objectives and success in all aspects of their personal and professional lives. When you properly manage all aspects of your life, you enjoy every single moment of it. Connect with Claude at www. ClaudeVigneault.com.

Tomoko Omori

"Impossible" Is just an Opinion

Imagine standing outside on a very windy day. How do you react to the weather? Do you complain about it? Or do you think, *The wind is beautiful. It makes me cool and it's a nice wind?* Just a little word, a *nice* wind, changes the whole perspective. And with a change in perception, your whole life can be brighter. The way you think can change your life and help you become successful. It has helped me, over and over again, in every situation I've encountered and every job I've ever had.

I came to America from Japan to study theater and become an actress. When I first arrived in California, I barely spoke English and it made me act shy and quiet. I never spoke to people. I even took classes in pantomime to avoid using English.

One of my teachers saw right through me, though. "Tomoko, why did you come to America?" he said. "If you don't at least try to challenge yourself, you should go back to Japan."

It was a hard truth to hear, but it made me think. I realized that staying quiet and avoiding what made me uncomfortable was not the way to go.

That was when I decided to never say *I cannot*—to never even think it. I realized that *hard* or *impossible* are just opinions. If I believe I can't do something, I won't be able to do it. If I think something is hard, it's going to be hard for me.

So I decided not to speak Japanese at all for two years. During that time, I avoided my Japanese colleagues or asked them to speak to me in English. I even asked my parents not to call me, so we only communicated through letters. It would have been so easy to make exceptions, but I was determined. And once I chose this harder way, life actually became much easier. Other students and actors were very helpful. People started to like me. I had a successful audition for a scholarship at an acting school in New York City.

Then, in 1996, something happened that changed my life. I had just received my immigration visa and was acting in an off-Broadway show. That day, my roommate had a friend over, so I left for the gym and then straight to the theater for a matinee show. I didn't even take my purse; all I had with me were my keys and a gym card. When I came back that evening, everything I owned was gone. The building we lived in had burned down. I lost everything—my clothes, my money, even the diaries that I had kept since I was eight.

It was an electrical fire, so there was no blaze, but the walls had become brittle and collapsed. Half of the L-shaped building was down and I could see the remaining section as if the building had been cut in half. My room was already gone; my roommate had

The way you think can change your life.

been evacuated. I saw our refrigerator hanging in the air on the third floor, and I heard someone yell, "Run! Run! It's gonna come down!"

All the firefighters spread away from the building just before the rest of it collapsed as though a bomb went off. Everything, even the refrigerator, became ash in a split second. Oddly enough, my roommate and I did not despair.

We were the only tenants who managed to stay positive. Since we were both actresses, we decided that going through all that—experiencing the fire, the loss, even fainting from shock—might be good for our acting.

But more than that, my life had become so much lighter. I had nothing to hide or protect anymore. I felt so open. Of course, I was blessed to have the support of people around me. My friends offered me a place to stay, clothes and financial help. Thanks to them, I was able to finish all my scheduled performances.

What stayed with me the most was a piece of advice: "Don't be a victim. You have to move on."

It helped me get back on my feet very quickly and I'm sure it was one of the reasons I didn't really take anything negative away from the fire.

Since that incident, everything changed. I wanted to give back. I wanted to help other people. Soon, I realized I had lost my passion for acting. I looked at life differently now—everyday life was drama enough. I didn't need to act or become someone else to be happy and fulfilled. As one of my mentors said when I told him my story, life itself became my stage. I quit acting and it's a change I don't regret. I enjoy life more now. I'm comfortable being myself and telling my own story, not someone else's.

I tried different things: working at the sports division of a Japanese TV network, selling advertisements, creating a magazine to introduce Japanese food and culture to New Yorkers. I didn't have any experience in any of those positions when I started but, with my passion, hard work and positive attitude, I succeeded in each of them within a few years.

Then I was offered a unique opportunity. Hirokazu Miyamori, the president of the Japanese Go!Go!Curry! chain of restaurants, was looking for someone to take over nationwide expansion in America after opening his first restaurant in New York. Go!Go!Curry! was one of the few companies that had grown during the recent recession. I had been helping them with advertisements and marketing for some time.

The first time I was offered the job, the magazine I'd created was still on the rocks. I turned down the offer. Three years later, when the magazine had become profitable and was in good hands, I was ready to move on and accept the new challenge.

I asked for six months' delay before starting the job—time to pass everything over to my successor—and I got it. The only condition was that the next restaurant be opened by May 5, 2012. That gave me a mere five months fom the moment I became president. It was a very short time, I knew—my husband was a restaurateur, too, and it took him a year and a half to open a restaurant. But I refused to think I couldn't do it. Impossible is just an opinion, after all. That belief helped me through the next months. I had to manage everything concerning the new restaurant, from location to

The building we lived in had burned down.

financing. While still working for the magazine, I started looking at properties, taking an hour here and there whenever I found an interesting location. I visited almost a hundred properties before I found the perfect one. It was December 2011.

I had five months until the deadline. However, we only got three months of free rent and, since I didn't want to pay rent without generating income, I decided we would open on March 15 instead. It didn't seem like a crazy idea then. Everyone kept saying we had so much time; even the construction company claimed we would be finished in a month. But as time passed and we were no closer to being ready, people started doubting we could do it.

"It's crazy to open in March," they said.

But I just told everyone, "I believe in you and I believe we can do it." I gave them that strong belief.

We still had a month and, even though things had been piling up and nothing was really happening, it was enough time to complete what needed to be done.

"You said we would be ready in a month," I reminded everyone. "We have a month. So let's do it."

We focused on getting one thing done every day. The rest could wait; focusing on one thing at a time, getting one step done each day, meant we were moving forward. Still, three days before opening, the restaurant seemed far from ready. But my conviction never faltered. I was there every day, reminding everyone that we were opening in three days, in two, tomorrow.

Then the big day came. That morning at seven, the whole staff was there, excited. We still didn't have gas, but it didn't matter. We had electricity, we had a roof over our heads, so no matter what, rain or shine, we would open. All the staff members got flyers to distribute: *We open today at ten; 55 cents per serving for the first 555 customers!* By nine, a line of people two blocks long waited for us to open. And at nine, our gas was finally connected. It seemed the universe was watching over us, wanting us to succeed.

I had imagined this moment for months, taking my strength from the vision of reaching my goal; I had pictured the lines;

If you don't believe, no one else will.

---

people cheering and smiling; my staff serving them food. Now that moment was a reality and I couldn't be happier. People kept congratulating me, especially those who had insisted that I wouldn't be able to open so soon. I was speechless from all the support. It was only the beginning of the restaurant, but we had reached an important goal. Even though more goals lay ahead, it was a memorable day. That night, we went to dinner to celebrate the success we had worked for so hard. After a whole day of serving people, my excitement still buzzed. But I was also exhausted. I fell asleep on the table after barely a few bites.

When I think about what the spirit of success is, I remember what it took to reach that goal: commitment to do whatever it takes to succeed and strong belief that it can be done. As a leader, you have to be a strong believer in what you're going to achieve. If you don't believe, no one else will and it's going to be a disaster. Stop thinking that something can't be done, that it's impossible or hard. If you think it's hard, it will be. But positive perception, hard work and firm belief in achieving your goal will get you anywhere.

Last year, I learned one more important thing about achieving goals. I ran the New York Marathon for the first time. I was scared that I wouldn't be able to finish it, but I imagined myself crossing that finish line with people cheering for me and it helped considerably. I did succeed. But what I learned was not about reaching that line—it was about getting there.

Halfway through the run, an older Japanese man I'd met injured himself. He wanted to finish the marathon nonetheless; I decided to keep him company and cheer him on. Running slowly next to him, without caring about speed and time as we talked, made me appreciate the simple joy of running. More speed could have killed that joy and make the marathon an ordeal. But when I knew I would reach my goal and let myself appreciate the process of getting there, it was fun.

So, as important as all those other things are—perspective, belief, hard work and moving forward—they are not *all*. Remember to take time to enjoy the process.

Many people give up before they fulfill their dreams or reach their goal—often *just* before they get there. They've been working so hard for so long and they are tired of it. It's hard to persevere sometimes, but try taking that one next step. Just one more. Imagine yourself reaching your goal—happiness, people cheering. It will be a reality if you keep moving forward. It will be worth it.

Tomoko Omori is the president of the New York subsidiary of a Japanese restaurant chain, Go!Go!Curry!USA, Inc. Tomoko came to the United States from Japan to become an actress and studied at Monterey Peninsula College in California and at the American Musical and Dramatic Academy in New York City. In 1996, just as her off-Broadway career was launching, she lost everything in an apartment fire. She moved on to work at the sport broadcasting production company of NHK-US, successfully sold advertisements during the recession and created a magazine about Japanese food and culture in New York. Connect with Tomoko at www.GoGoCurryUSA-NY.com.

Carey Buck

STOP ASKING PERMISSION

W hen my wife, Kathy, asked me one day, "Why don't you ask your boss if you can go part-time so that you can concentrate more on our businesses?" I swear I almost fell off my chair. "We're never gonna get further if you keep working forty hours a week, coming home tired and sleepy," she added.

The expression on my face must have been priceless—this was all coming from a woman who has always been an "employee," working in a job that she loves with all the security that brings. What I did—and had almost always done—was work a straight job but having entrepreneurial side hustles.

Frankly, it scared the crap out of her. Yet here she was, telling me I should work less at my job and focus more on our own business ventures—because it's hard to be successful in your own business when you're working what feels like a million hours a week and then coming home to a family. It's doable—just really hard. I didn't really stop to question it—she was the only person with whom I'd ever been in a relationship who ever believed in me.

"You can do it," she told me and I thought, *I have to do this now—for her. I have to get off my butt and do this.*

Not long ago, when I had asked for a day off, I'd heard, "Sorry, but we just can't spare you."

I had thought then, *I have to ask permission from somebody I couldn't care less about to spend more time with somebody who means the world to me. This is* crazy. *Why would anybody do this? I shouldn't have to ask permission to spend quality time with my family. I'm gonna make sure this never happens again.*

Now, with Kathy's encouragement, on Monday, I asked my boss straight out, "Can I go part-time?"

She was awesome and really supportive of what I was doing. I'd never kept my side ventures a secret and she knew my ultimate goal was to not work there. Going part-time wasn't a problem—I asked for what I wanted and I got it! My boss was on board and, man, I started kicking tail when I went part-time. Between working on our ATM business, making offers on apartment buildings and improving my information marketing course so that others could start making passive income from ATM machines, I was crushing it and taking names.

For all of about a month, that is. It was June 2012; Kathy and I were gearing up for summer break, feeling fantastic since I'd be home to watch Joe, my stepson. That made things so much simpler!

And then my boss called me in, looking sheepish. "We need you to come back full-time again," she told me. "I know it's not

---

I asked my boss straight out, "Can I go part-time?"

---

good timing. I wish you were just ready to leave and be on your own, but we're getting busier and busier and we need you."

At first, I didn't know what to say. *It's only been a month. A month! But okay. Cool. She's running a business; she has to ask the question.*

"Take the weekend to think about it and talk it over with Kathy," she asked and I agreed.

It was a tough decision. When I was a small child, I would watch family and neighbors get up every morning and work between forty and seventy hours a week at jobs they hated. They only looked forward to one day a week: Friday. "Thank God it's Friday," they'd all say. The confusing part as a kid was that, once Friday came around, they dreaded one other day: Monday. I realized as a kid that I was different and that I didn't just want to look forward to one day a week every week for the rest of my life.

My mom always, *always,* told me, "Carey, you can be whatever you want to be and do whatever you want to do in your life. You just have to get out there and *do* it."

Eventually I realized how I was different—I wanted to be an entrepreneur. In my late teens and early twenties I kept trying to start businesses—even a psychic hotline! But I was a kid; I didn't know what the hell I was doing! Sure, some money was coming in,

I pulled out all the stops to up my game.

but I had no idea how to run a really profitable business. I always had to make money and everyone around me was making their money by having a job.

I might have had the entrepreneurial bug, but I still had to eat; I ended up stuck in the "Thank God it's Friday/ugh, I'm not looking forward to Monday" grind. I worked all sorts of jobs, but I knew none of them were what I really wanted and I was a pretty bad employee. No kidding, I hated getting up and going to work so much that I was late every day. Some part of me was probably thinking, *If you're late, maybe they'll fire you and then you can get the lead out and do what you need to do,* with another part of me saying, *Can you really make it, though? Can you do it on your own?*

When I next spoke to my boss after talking it over with Kathy, I said, "I can come back full-time in September if you need me, once Joe has gone back to school."

At that point, we'd already made plans and, what with summer clubs filling up, it was damn near impossible to change them. But my boss told me, "We can't wait until then; we need you now."

I said, "Okay, no problem, I understand—but I can't do that because of Joe. Our plan was for me to be home this summer."

It was go back full-time or be let go—and it was Kathy who said, "Well, I guess you can't go back."

My boss understood and June 8, 2012, was my official last day as an employee of someone else. Man, did it feel awesome! The next morning I woke up feeling energized and ready to be what I wanted to be and do what I needed to do—as Mom always told me, I just had to get out there and *do* it.

After leaving my job, I pulled out all the stops to up my game. *Okay, I have forty hours in a week to do whatever the hell I need to*

Fulfilling a dream was incredible.

---

do for my *business, finally.* The tricky part was *how* to divvy up my time, because we had two businesses—the ATM business and the information marketing business. After looking at everything, I put the ATM business on the backburner for a while so that I could focus more on the information marketing. I loved the feeling I got when I would speak with people or meet people at events and they would say, "This really helped me! It got me thinking and changed my life!"

No longer was it just the daily grind to make the money—I was making money in a way that gave me satisfaction and allowed me to spend more time with the people I love *and* I didn't have to ask permission to do a damn thing. I wanted to concentrate my efforts on helping other people realize that they have this choice as well.

It is hard; you need to act as though you're at a job, *really* work eight hours a day and plan your day. Your vision will be much bigger than that, but you do need to take it day by day as well. It takes some time—few people can just do what they need to do right away and no "overnight success" really happened overnight. For me, it was a long internal battle before I was finally able to make that choice and say, "You know what? Screw this. I'm not going back to work; *this* is how I want to live the rest of my life." It takes some figuring out and a hell of a lot of discipline, because there's nobody you have to ask for permission—apart from yourself.

Before I made the shift, working was horrible—I wasn't miserable, but I wasn't happy in all areas of my life. Kathy knew that I was unhappy in a job—you can tell when something is missing from somebody. Sunday would come around and I was miserable because all I could think was, *Oh, back to work tomorrow.*

Now, I feel free. It's stressful sometimes and I had to get really tough with myself in the beginning, because it takes a *lot* of discipline to get up in the morning and not just bum around the house. But overall, there is absolutely no comparison whatsoever. You feel free; you're finally doing what you're supposed to do, really living your passion. It's a feeling that I would never want to lose again.

Way back in 2009, I had attended the Peak Potentials Never Work Again seminar, which is all about passive income ideas. Even though I had no idea how, or even what, I'd speak about, at the end of that seminar, I wrote in their questionnaire, *I want to be speaking on your stage one day.* In November 2012, I spoke on the Never Work Again stage for the first time—it was the first speaking engagement of that magnitude I'd ever had. It was an incredible feeling to share how I'd made a choice that is available to everyone—settle for the daily grind or get out there and *do* it, whatever "it" is—and how I was fulfilling my dream.

As a full-time entrepreneur, I can say that I honestly look forward to every single day—even Monday! What kinds of successes could you achieve if you stopped asking for permission, got out there and *did* it?

Carey Buck is the CEO and founder of the ATM Business Blueprint Success System. She has spent the last twenty years designing and developing a massive passive income system that will allow you to achieve financial freedom. As a successful entrepreneur, Carey is committed to helping others realize that they don't have to work forty to seventy hours a week for their entire lives at jobs they hate—real, attainable options are out there for them and they have a choice in life! For your next steps, connect with Carey at www.GoinFlippinCrazy. com. and at www.ATMBusinessBlueprint.com.

Mara Hoover

On Your Terms

Speaking to a large group didn't faze me; I majored in public speaking in college. But when I looked over the audience of seventy women assembled for my first seminar and saw that they were nearly twice my age, I had a moment of doubt. *Will they believe that I, a twenty-nine year old blonde, can help them create a life that they absolutely love? What will they think when I suggest that they revisit their childhood dreams? Will they trust me when I ask them to rewrite their money soundtracks?*

I took a deep breath and stepped out. I heard a rustle from the audience as I began speaking. I looked at the faces before me, seeing a mixture of doubt and hope. As I continued, I noticed more and more people were leaning over notebooks. Soon all the women were scribbling madly. *They trust me; they hear me; they believe me! What an incredible feeling!*

"How does such a young woman become a financial expert, equipping other women with the tools to redefine and reinvent themselves and to create what they truly want in their lives?" you ask.

I began setting big goals early. When I was five, I announced, "I'm going to see all seven continents and write a book and have a million dollars, all before I'm thirty."

My parents, bless them, didn't laugh. We were an entrepreneurial family, so my parents encouraged me to set big goals and work to achieve them. Unlike most families, we talked about money. From the time I was little, Dad would sit down with me and pull out white printer paper and write out as he spoke, "Okay, if you save ten dollars each month from your allowance and it earns ten percent interest, next year you'll have this much. The next year, you earn interest on the total and, if you save another ten dollars per month, you have that much. Then you start saving twenty-five dollars and then you start saving a hundred dollars and by the time you hit fifty, you'll be a millionaire." Being a millionaire always made mathematical sense to me.

Dad had a construction business, which, of course, had ups and downs. I knew we were in a "poor spell" when we had crappy cars, like the neon-green Geo Metro covered in dents that only seated four—there were five of us. When money was tight, Mom sewed my school clothes. On top of that, I had a very crooked tooth and

Unlike most families, we talked about money.

Mom cut my hair in a mullet—it was easier for me to manage. With all those quirky traits, it was seemingly inevitable that I was teased by other girls at school. I spent a lot of time standing alone in the corner of the playground or hiding out in the library. It was better to be alone than to be teased.

As I grew up, I embraced my eccentric qualities and grew to love myself, although I didn't feel the same way about the girls who had teased me. To reach my big childhood dreams—and, honestly, to avoid women—I started working in Dad's construction business (no women there!) when I was sixteen and began saving in a 401(k) right away. I led my first construction projects the summer I was seventeen.

After college, I didn't want to see the family company go to someone who wouldn't understand and share the vision Dad had worked so hard to build over the last twenty-five years. He had always let me know that stepping into the business was an option. So I eagerly joined the family business.

In early 2008, we were a seven million dollar construction company, sizeable for a local market. I was vice president and owned half the stock. I had diligently saved eighty thousand dollars in my 401(k). I had my own stockbroker, and made all of my own investment decisions. I was newly married and was finally a homeowner. Dad was two months away from semi-retirement. He had saved his entire life so that he could travel around the world and do construction work for mission projects in third world countries. Everything was going according to plan.

Mid-October, in what seemed like the blink of an eye, all of that disappeared. Dad lost half of his 401(k) savings, multiple six-figures, and had to use the rest of his money to keep the company

---

Losing half your money gives you perspective.

---

afloat, which shrank from seven million in revenue to less than half a million in revenue by the following year. I had to lay off twenty of our twenty-four employees. Personally, I lost half of my family income, half of my retirement savings and worked with no salary for a whole year. My new husband and I had to short-sell our house, losing about two hundred thousand dollars. Adding to the already challenging situation, Mom decided she was no longer fulfilled in her relationship and felt a lack of connectedness in her marriage. So Mom and Dad divorced.

It all happened so fast that it was shocking. In just six months, so many pieces of my life were falling apart. I realized that if I stayed in the family business, my dad was going to pay me a salary that he really didn't have; every dollar he paid me would cut into his ability to retire. I said, "Dad, if I leave, you can build the company back up and sell it; maybe you can recoup some of your losses."

For so many years, I had thought my future was running the family business. *Now what am I going to do with my life?* Then I realized, When you look at all the pieces of your life and all of your expectations shattered and piled on the floor, you have only two choices; you can wallow in "what was" for the rest of your life, or you can hit the reset button and start over, rebuild and keep dreaming. I tried a couple of business ventures while transitioning out of the family business. A vacation rental concierge business demanded way too much labor. Of course, I did the stint of network marketing that seems to be required of entrepreneurs. All the while, I continued my search for a place where I could put my money and not lose. After losing half of my 401k, forty thousand

You can create an incredible life.

dollars, to be exact, I wanted a new solution. When you are young, most people say you can afford the risk, so you should take it; but losing half your money gives you perspective. I was searching, but what I didn't realize was that I would find a great financial solution and a new career along the way.

Either my broker didn't know what safe options existed, or he wasn't telling. Then, through divine synchronicity, I met a couple, Chris and Denise, from Five Rings Financial and that "chance" meeting changed the trajectory of my life forever. They spoke about growing money in a safe environment, earning decent interest without all the risk of the stock market. Wow! That was my cup of tea. I decided to launch into a career with Five Rings Financial and quickly became its youngest executive vice president. I became a leader and facilitator in our Wine, Women and Wealth events. Meeting and sharing with amazing women at those events started to heal a lot of the wounds from being teased in school.

Seeing how resilient women are and the creative ideas they come up with to create businesses gave me the impetus to move past my childhood pain and truly support and empower women. With my new-found love for women and a deeper understanding of my mom's journey, I founded FemmePowerU in the summer of 2013 to create a space for women to celebrate and embody what makes them unique and equip them with a basic understanding of money and how they could use it achieve their definition of success.

Success is a fascinating word. Often, we just allow an assumed definition to take over our lives and so we're often aiming for something we don't even want. Defining success for yourself is the most important first step. Are you a great mother? Are you great in business, or a great wife, or a great employee? What do you want your life to look like? Put your own goals into place so that, when you achieve them, you can celebrate who you are and what you've accomplished.

Success is one of those charged words, which, if you don't define it for yourself, can haunt you for the rest of your life, because you think you have to live up to someone else's expectations. I was blessed to create my own success definition as a young child and despite all of the teasing and not fitting in, I held fast to my dreams, on my terms!

When it's your expectations, and you give yourself permission to define what it means to you, you can create an incredible life, because you're accomplishing what you want. And at the end of the day, being self-centered or selfish, if you will, is one of the most important things women can do because, if we don't take care of ourselves, we can't show up for everyone else who depends on us.

I'm proud to say that I am well on my way toward meeting the goals that defined success for me when I was five. I released my first book when I was twenty five.

People said, "You don't have a book deal."

I replied, "I don't care, I'll print it myself."

I wanted to get my story and my ideas out into the world. For me, that was success; I don't have to sell a million copies. I'm twenty-nine and I only have two continents, Asia and Australia, left to visit and a trip booked for September to check them off my list. My new goal is to visit every continent as an invited speaker, without having any expense.

I've recouped my financial losses and am on my way to my million dollars. I expect to reach all my childhood goals. And then, I'll say, "Hey, I'm only thirty. What's next? What other wild ideas can I come up with that I can achieve?

Now, when I speak before a group of women about rewriting their money soundtracks so that they too can live a life that meets their *own* expectations, there is no voice of doubt. My message is what all women—all people, really—want and need to hear: It's never too early to pursue a long-held dream, to secure the bright, beautiful future you envisioned. And if you set that dream aside, know that it's never too late to pick it back up, dust it off and make it happen. It's your turn!.

Mara Hoover is on a mission to empower women to gain financial literacy, confront their fears, eliminate guilt and move forward in life with a plan that works. Resonating with the message of Five Rings Financial, she joined the team and in two short years she became the youngest executive vice president. As founder of FemmePowerU and FinancialPowerU, Mara is passionate about empowering women and entrepreneurs to find fulfillment and financial freedom on their terms. Hang on to your hat, not hers, as Mara shares how you can tune in and tune up your money soundtrack to propel you toward the wealth and lifestyle you deserve.

Mara wrote My Grumpy Husband *in 2011 and is set to release* Throw the Fear Overboard! *In spring 2014. To learn more about Mara Hoover and her companies, please visit: www.MaraHoover.com, www. FemmePowerU.com and www.FinancialPowerU.com.*

Pam Macdonald

No Regrets

One night about four years into our relationship, the love of my life took me to task and gave me an ultimatum. In my role as senior project manager for an international company, I had been working punishing eighty-hour weeks for more than six months, sacrificing time with Peter, time for myself and time for anything outside of work.

I had camped out at the kitchen table with my laptop, intent on working into the evening. The bathroom was off limits due to a tile regrouting project and I was tense because it was my only window to have a shower for the next thirty hours. So when Peter approached me, I reacted badly, as if to say, *Oh great—now what?*

It must have been the last straw because my normally gentle, non-confrontational partner suddenly said, "Do you realize that you are not a nice person when you work like this? This job is making you a different person, and I'm not even sure I like the person you are right now."

Shocked, I looked up from my laptop and into Peter's eyes. I opened my mouth and closed it, unable to find words to express how hurt I was by his admission. Though I was proud of him for finding the courage to be honest with me, I was devastated. And I was frightened, because in that moment it was as if everything I held dear was likely to go.

I thought, *I might lose this amazing person in my life and if I do, it would be my fault.* In about two seconds I realized that I had the power to do something differently and yet, time and time again, had chosen work over Peter and over my own needs. *You need a wakeup call and here it is.*

I had been working in a way that was unsustainable; I knew I couldn't keep it up for the next two years, let alone ten. I'd put so much into my career that I'd forgotten the important things and people in my life. At times, I can be like a steamroller, or a

---

Everything I held dear was likely to go.

---

tank, or a fireball—or all three, rolled into one! I had been working hard, long hours, letting my high-level job transform me. It was such a challenging situation, and it took such bravery for Peter to confront me. For me, he was saying, "Look lady, I love you and I really care for you, but I'm not going to let myself be treated badly."

Finally I found my voice, "Wow! That's hard to hear and I must have needed to hear it, so I appreciate you telling me. I want to be the type of person you want to be around." I took a deep breath and asked the big question. "Do I have time to make this right?"

"Yeah, not a lot of time," Peter replied.

My heart quickened; it was not the response I was hoping to hear. I closed my laptop and said, "Could I have a hug?"

Of course he said yes and, as Peter's arms wrapped tightly around me, I made a silent vow to handle my life very, very differently. From that moment forward I began mapping out a plan to meet my work obligations but not be so horrid about it. More than that, I started looking for an exit strategy.

I was raised with the traditional view that if you're a good person and you work hard, you'll get the right results. For most of my life I believed this was the correct path to success. So I played by the rules and I worked really, really hard. My career path had been diligent and upwardly mobile—I always expected to gain a new skill and experience with each role.

This strategy worked pretty well for a while; I worked for several blue chip corporations in financial and professional services, ending up in my senior project manager position overseeing work in seventeen countries. Most people would have considered my life a success. And yet, while I was being amazingly productive and delivering great work, I was becoming someone I didn't recognize.

In the past, I had looked to some of my managers as my key influence points. After Peter expressed his feelings about the woman I had become while on the path to "success," I realized that, if working all hours at the expense of my heart, my interests, my own health and well-being was what success looked like, I wanted to opt out. *That's not how I want people to remember me. That's not how I want to live my life.*

Once I made the commitment to change my ways, I took action pretty quickly. Thanks to Peter's honesty, I was conscious and aware and that is always the best place to begin. I couldn't immediately change my workload without having a negative impact on our finances; I *could* change, I *did* change, where I focused my attention when not at work. I made sure that when I was with Peter, I was truly *with him*. And I took time to explore what I truly wanted out of life—to redefine success on my own terms.

At times I did grow frustrated because it seemed change was happening too slowly. I wanted to fix everything straight away, but that's not possible. When you're in a routine with deadlines and commitments, you can't turn off the tap and be done with it. It was a process of adjustment. We made progress and after another six months Peter and I were able to go on a three month holiday together. Though I wasn't sure we could get there, our relationship has gone into a deeper level of trust and connection.

As I adjusted my habits to achieve balance in my personal life, professional life transformed as well. I began to see how my unique skill set, expertise and personal experience could be of tremendous value to other people and businesses in periods of transition, so I set up my own consulting business guiding individuals and organizations in their own journeys through transformational change. Right from the first month, I've been comfortable saying "no" to certain types of work when it is not consistent with who I am or who I want to be. And right from the start I have believed I've been living my purpose—even when money was not as plentiful as it had been. I know that I feel and behave more in tune with who I really am than I had in a very, very long time.

When I work with clients, I assist them in managing themselves and their careers in a way that is consistent with these four fundamentals: results, relationships, rapport and reputation. As I

I was becoming someone I didn't recognize.

---

had to learn the hard way, a successful career is much, much more than the results you can deliver. Sure, results are important and yet it is also essential to be clear on how you got those results. The corporate world has too many collateral casualties, the people who have been pushed and pressured aside or into a breakdown so that someone else can have "success."

Success is also about the relationships you can build, which are closely linked to *how* you get your results. An old African proverb says, "To go fast, go alone; to go far, take others with you." And this is the heart of what I am aiming at: we need to build good relationships with others at work and at home. Human beings are fundamentally tribal creatures; we want to fit in and to be valued.

Building good strong relationships relies on treating people well and taking them on the journey with you, not trampling them underfoot or brushing them aside while you surge ahead.

Rapport with others is often described as the skill of managing different stakeholders, yet it is also about who we are when we connect with others. There are many words for it—authentic, genuine, respectful, nice—yet rapport is also about understanding how we want to interact with others and then adapting in order to achieve that outcome.

Lastly, it's about your reputation. Because your reputation is something that you carry everywhere with you, your reputation is like trust—painstaking to build yet easy to fracture. Your reputation is a result of the other fundamentals and it is also something on which we often ignore feedback, or write off the feedback of others thinking they are jealous or don't understand! For example, if you throw yourself into your work so much so that you repeatedly get sick, that cycle of work-sick, work-sick can damage the way you are perceived in your industry.

Today I live by the philosophy of "no regrets." When I get to the end of my life, whether it's next week, or next year, or in sixty years, I want to look back on my life and say, *I don't regret anything that I did or the way I did it.* Sure I may reflect, *If I knew then what I know now, I may have made a different choice* because everything

---

To go far, take others with you.

---

in life teaches us something when we are ready to learn and willing to listen to the lessons around us. I'm so glad that I did.

Success is different for everybody. I look around me and see people with the material trappings of success carrying around empty and pain-filled hearts. When I defined success on my own terms it became about being able to do fulfilling work and help others in a way that was sustainable for me, for my health and well-being, for my primary relationship and to be nicely present with other family and friends. For some people, success may be financial freedom to choose when they do or don't do things, but my simpler definition of success ultimately leads me to that outcome. However you define success, remember that it is more about how we live our whole lives, not just our work.

If you feel out of sync or off balance, it might be time to think about how you define success. The spirit or essence of who we are speaks loudly to others; when we are out of alignment with our spirit or purpose, it will be clear to those around us. When Peter expressed his unhappiness with my behavior and actions, he was picking up on the fact that something wasn't quite right with me. Humans are usually pretty good at sensing that disconnect. The trouble is, we are often unable to articulate that discomfort or clarify it so we can understand. And if you are also dealing with limiting self-beliefs, it is all too easy to be swayed or influenced by someone at work, even if somewhere in your being something seems off-kilter or wrong.

If you've lost a piece of yourself or your serenity on your own path to success, if your relationships or passions have suffered because you're disconnected from your spirit or purpose, take heart. I am living proof that transformation is possible, on your own terms, and in your own time.

Begin by stepping off the treadmill of life and taking a deep breath. Next, look around and ask yourself the question, "Is this what I really want? Is this the life that's right for me?" Then, check in with someone you trust who remembers who you really are. Ask them, "Am I behaving in ways that I can always be proud of?"

When we connect with the core of who we are, the rest of life is easier to manage: work/life balance, self-care, healthy relationships, satisfying work, dreams fulfilled.

Work is an important part of life, but it doesn't have to be horrid and hard. You can do it in a way that works for you if you make sure that you focus not only on what you're doing, but on who you are becoming while you're doing it. Then, when you look back on your beautiful life, you can do so without regret.

Pam Macdonald is a senior human resources and change management professional with diverse and extensive experience gained from working in the public and private sectors. She works with individuals and organizations to support, guide and assist their journeys through transformational change. Her ability to develop and implement effective and pragmatic strategies is due to her strong analytical ability and the credibility her personal career experience engenders. Pam has had deep exposure to a wide range of people, business and development initiatives and, having led the human relations function within the banking sector, is well positioned to ensure that outcomes deliver on commercial, cultural and people dimensions. Pam has worked in a broad range of industries including electricity, consulting, financial services and retail and professional services in both line and project management roles. This breadth of experience in functional and industry spheres gives her a unique perspective. Her collaborative style ensures that she effectively engages stakeholders and facilitates ownership of outcomes by designated stakeholders. She is currently chair of the Bendigo Cemeteries Trust, a board member of the Central Victorian Community Foundation and a member of the National Executive Committee of the Career Development Association of Australia. Connect with Pam at www.PamMacdonald.com.

John Long

CAN'T IS A COWARD'S WORD

I t wouldn't start! The semi in which I had invested so much work, so much hope and so much money just sat there. I banged my fists on the steering wheel. *What do I do now? I don't even have enough money to fix the starter.*

I remembered all the long, lonely nights sitting in motels, waiting, waiting, waiting for a load to take from Dallas, Texas to Alberta, Canada and then back to Vancouver. Loads of lumber from Vancouver to Texas were easy to come by, but the oil industry in Alberta was in a slump and finding a load of oil drilling equipment had been getting harder every trip. For two years now, money had been getting more scarce and hotel rooms had been getting more lonely. But I had to wait for a load. Going home empty would cost a fortune in diesel fuel.

Other truckers found solace and companionship in local bars. But drinking is just waste of money that will kill your brain and spirit. So, alone in a strange city, I'd kill some time polishing my truck and then sit in my room watching television, enduring that terrible feeling of helplessness, waiting for someone to have a load for me.

I'd already used up my savings. I had no money for truck maintenance and the other bills were piling up. My wife, Claire, was doing in-home daycare to help make ends meet. As my independent trucking business slid downhill, Claire had been my staunch support. But she cried a lot and she had gained weight. Stress was taking its toll on both of us.

And now the doggone truck wouldn't start! In utter despair, I climbed out of my truck and walked away. I called the bank to tell them where the truck was so they could repossess it. Bankruptcy was the only way out of debt.

My friends said, "Oh, no, you'll never find a job if you file for bankruptcy." But I would have had to borrow from friends or relatives and I didn't want to do that. I'd blown all my own money and I didn't want to start spending money that belonged to other people.

How would I support my wife and young children?

I made good money as an independent trucker the first year. I was on top of the world, making my own decisions. *I can do what I want to do and my money is mine to do with as I like. I'm the master of my own fate.* But then interest rates went up and business slowed down. I was underfinanced, because I didn't know enough about business to have a cash reserve for slow periods. And now I was bankrupt. How would I support my wife and young children?

At first I didn't want to talk to people, even friends. I was embarrassed; it seemed as though I'd really gone down in the world. My Grandma Ann's words came to me: "Can't is a coward's word; always say, 'I'll try.'" She was raised in a log cabin with a dirt floor and never went to school a day in her life. But she taught herself to read using the Bible, the only book in the house. She taught herself; not just basic arithmetic, but eventually bookkeeping so she could help her husband in his sawmill business. Grandma Ann was a strong, self-made woman and I'd been lucky to spend so much time with her.

Her words, her example, had helped me before. When I was fifteen, I broke my neck. Physiotherapy fifty years ago wasn't as good as it is now, and I faced life as a cripple. But "can't is a coward's word." I kept trying various things, doing what had to be done to build up my strength and finally healed myself.

At this new low point, her words echoed. I realized: *I'm not my work, I'm me.*

One lovely day in July, I was out for a walk and heard, "What the hell is your problem?"

I was startled to see Rollie, my former partner in a log-recovery business. I told my story. He had a problem, too. He didn't have a part-time driver he trusted and was working seven days a week. He offered me a job driving Friday, Saturday and Sunday evenings.

After the first weekend, I realized I could make enough to pay for rent and groceries. Through another friend, I found a second part-time job driving the bus for a private school and a third cleaning the school gymnasium after Saturday night dances. Claire found part-time work as a clerk in a bakery. We lost our house and

> ***Now we knew we could overcome
> anything life threw at us.***

moved into a rental unit in a duplex. But I was paying my bills. I didn't go on social assistance. With my wife, I kept things together and supported my family; our little children were fed, clothed, loved and looked after.

We held our own until the recession eased and my former company hired me back as a mechanic. Claire took a full-time job as a payroll clerk in an iron foundry. I designed a house for us and built it on a shoestring after a sympathetic banker gave me credit based on my work ethic. A couple of friends with pickup trucks helped us move our bits of furniture, but walking in the door of our own home once again was a glorious feeling. We had not only survived, we had dug ourselves out of a deep hole. Now we knew we could overcome anything life threw at us.

Claire and I retired a year ago. We both have good pensions, so I have no need to work. But I got bored being a couch potato and, half from curiosity, half from boredom, went to a self-help seminar. I was hooked and became a "seminar junkie."

I realized that I have something important to share. If Grandma Ann could educate herself and if I could dig myself out of bankruptcy, then there's no excuse, no problem too big to overcome.

I've made it my business to seek out the folks who have answers and inspiration so that I can connect people who need help with the best resource for them.

I was able to turn my life around because I am willing to do whatever it takes. I didn't stay at home and whine; I got out and talked to people even though I was embarrassed about my situation. That is why opportunities presented themselves.

> *If you're out there doing something and getting ahead, you're successful.*

You have to decide what you want, because success isn't just about money. Grandma Ann had a successful life although she was never wealthy—you're reading this book, so you already have a head start on her. I'm not a millionaire, but I raised happy, well-adjusted children and was successful in providing for them even during hard times.

If aren't going right or you've made a mistake, it doesn't mean you can sit around feeling sorry for yourself and say, "Oh, my gosh, the world is picking on me. I can't get ahead because 'they' won't let me." What the heck do you mean by "they?" You're a part of "they." You have to pull up your own socks and try things for yourself. Compared to how I grew up, I'm far ahead in life, way farther than I ever expected to be. I've seen how far people can get to and I want get farther.

Success is a process. If you're out there doing something and getting ahead, you're successful. You don't need a million dollars to be successful. If you're getting ahead in life and you're happy, I think you're fairly successful. I know musicians who play in local bands and make a good living; they're successful. They've never had an album go platinum; they're not millionaires or famous worldwide, but they're successful people. I think about local tradesmen, who have looked after their money properly so they have a house and income—they're successful people.

If you start investing or get a product and sell it and make a hundred thousand dollars a year, you're very successful. If you can raise that to a million dollars, maybe you are more successful; but you probably can't spend a million a year anyway. You don't need it to be happy or to define yourself as a success. You do have to be busy, active and useful to be successful.

When I was younger, I defined success as having money and the things money could buy; I thought everything else, including happiness, would come along automatically. Now I define success as having balance in my life in all areas. Success includes having stable relationships with family and with friends, balance at work, at play and in my spiritual life. Success is being satisfied in my financial life and having fun moving to the next level. Maybe that seems like an impossible dream, but "can't is a coward's word."

Tell me you'll try, too.

John Long is a retired mechanic who, at age sixty-six, is building a new career as a speaker and a guide to self-help resources for people who seek a solution to their problems and are willing to try. He's also been a partner in a log-salvage business and an independent trucker. John lives in Vancouver with his wife, Claire.

Sally F. Larson

Life Can Change in a Moment

Without warning, life almost ended for me over a decade ago in a horrific auto accident. It happened in November of 2001 while traveling with my husband, two children and my parents from Connecticut to Florida to go on a Thanksgiving cruise. In Florence, South Carolina on Route 95, two vehicles rolled over without touching while trying to avoid each other. The front-seat passenger in both vehicles perished; the drivers came out nearly unscathed.

My mom, who was the driver, and my son were bruised; my dad perished; and my husband, daughter and I were in intensive care with many complications. I have no memories from one month before and two months after the incident; and I really and truly don't want to know all the things that were wrong with me and my body. I do know that I had lots of broken bones, a collapsed lung, a punctured bladder and shattered pelvis and that my life was touch and go for quite a while. But the major long-lasting issue is my traumatic brain injury (TBI). For me, life as I knew it stopped the moment of the accident. My life was forever changed.

Once stabilized, I was airlifted to Gaylord Rehabilitation Hospital in Connecticut—the same facility where the "Central Park jogger" went to relearn everything after her attack—so that I could relearn how to drink, eat, walk and talk with the aid of occupational therapy, physical therapy, speech therapy and more. My earliest memory after the accident was waking up in a hospital net bed at Gaylord; it was a cage secured to the top of the bed with net on its sides and top. Nurses would zip open the net to check me and take my vitals and to offer me food and drink. I remember trying desperately to get my finger between the zipper pieces to open it. All I wanted was to get out of that bed and cage.

And I remember saying to a close friend, "Bring your ladder because I need to break out!"

After nearly twenty-five years in corporate America, where I had managed teams and complicated, high-level IT projects, suddenly I had to learn how to compensate for limitations I never expected to have. I knew in my head how to do things, but when I tried to do them, I could not. Before the accident I was a very intense, on-

---

Life as I knew it stopped.

---

task, type-A person. Having to ask for help because I could not remember how to do even the most basic things was difficult; I'm not one to ask for help. But I just kept reminding myself, *You can do this. Anything is possible. Maybe I can't do it the way I think I remember how to do it, but I can do it.*

In the mid-nineties I had discovered the Law of Attraction and came to understand that I could create my own destiny with my thoughts and feelings. I'm so grateful I discovered this law of the universe before the accident because, had I not had the belief that anything is possible, I would probably have had a much different outcome after my accident. I would have been a victim, not a survivor. I would have given in to frustration and let pain and vertigo and limitations control my life.

My mind was such a mess; I couldn't think straight. I would forget things that happened in the short-term. After I finally got my cell phone, I would call my husband from the rehab hospital and ask him where he was and when he was coming.

He would say, "I'm on my way home. I just left the hospital."

Some weeks after I finally returned home I felt more settled, as though I was coming back to who I was supposed to be, but I still had many challenges and many things to relearn. If you look at me today, you would think I sound fine and look fine; most people don't realize I had a head injury. Still, I had to come to terms with the fact that I would have to deal with the effects of TBI for the rest of my life. Everything takes me longer. I spend so much time looking for things I just had in my hand! Sometimes I felt broken, like damaged goods, but I just kept reminding myself, "Anything is possible."

Before the accident I was goal- and results-oriented. But after the accident, tangible results were no longer at the top of my list. I couldn't go back into corporate America, so I did a lot of self-examination and decided to find out who I was. *What is it that I really love? What is it that I really want?* I was searching and searching, training with the best thought leaders and personal development teachers in the world.

It took me almost a decade of trying different things to figure out what I wanted. It all changed when I found *The Passion Test,* a

---

Love is a decision, not just a feeling.

---

simple yet powerful process developed by Janet Bray Attwood that helped me clarify what was important to me. That's when things really started changing, because, once you're clear, things just start showing up. Miracles started occurring around me. I began living life to the fullest, so excited about helping others find and live their passions, to encourage and uplift people to be who they want to be. This is what I do best because I am *living proof* that anything *is* possible.

My husband jokes that he likes me better now than he did before the accident because I'm more relaxed. I go with the flow. Rather than falling back on my analytical mind and ego, I try to quiet my mind and listen from within for answers. My life is so much more joyous and complete since I made the shift to adjust my thinking.

There are no medicines to take or processes to follow—all I have to do is stop, evaluate and adjust my attitude, align with love and choose in favor of what matters most to me. I try to remember that it doesn't matter if I'm right or not. It only matters if I'm coming from a place of love. Love is a decision, not just a feeling. And it's my conscious choice to come from love.

All of the answers are within each of us. Our souls know. We just have to sit and listen and be open to receive whatever comes to us. If I'm unclear what I'm feeling, often I will ask the angels (guides, saints, and so on) to assist me. I quiet myself, and then begin by sending off appreciation and thanks. Since thanks and gratitude are lower vibrations and everything is energy and vibration, I

Do the scary impossible thing.

---

always try to give appreciation which is a higher vibration. Then I ask the angels for help and guidance. There are all kinds of angels; Archangel Michael is with us at all times. Or I might think about people who have crossed over, my ancestors.

I ask all the angels or a specific angel to assist me, knowing that angels can't help us unless we ask them. I ask for assistance and try not to be tied to the outcome. In the end I always say, "This or something better, for the highest good of all parties involved." Then I say, "I appreciate you and your help" and close with: "I send you love and light with great appreciation. I am open to receive."

While I still deal with the effects of my brain injury, I don't let it get in my way. I can't do the work I used to do; it's too much of a strain and I just can't keep track of thing as I used to. I tend to make mistakes. But I'm learning not to beat up on myself. I'm learning to accept who I am, just as I am. I always say, "Anything is possible." I don't get bothered when things come up, And because I believe it, and say it, and act on it, so it is.

Last year I went skydiving with a friend. I was the ninetieth jumper that day. I remember being strapped so tightly to my tandem partner I could feel him breathing. In the seconds after we jumped from the plane, I couldn't breathe because the wind force was so intense on my face. When the chute came up, it took the pressure off and I could breathe again. Gliding, gliding, gliding down to the ground, I looked below and saw what looked like a little ant world, immersed in gorgeous fall colors. It was incredible to be able to experience that. My heart was full of gratitude and appreciation for that moment and every moment that brought me to this joyous experience.

Anything is possible. Even if people tell you they think your ideas are crazy, remember that you are always taken care of. Do the scary impossible thing. You're not doing it alone.

Sally F. Larson is a certified passion test facilitator (trained by Janet Bray Attwood), an Interior Alignment™ instinctive feng shui/space cleaning practitioner, a soul coaching© practitioner and master soul coaching© oracle card practitioner (trained by Denise Linn), and an angel card practitioner (certified by Doreen Virtue and Raleigh Valentine). Sally helps people get in touch with what's important to them and, when faced with decisions or opportunities, learn how to live their lives passionately by consciously choosing in favor of their passions.

Sally has had extensive trainings with Deepak Chopra and the Chopra Center; Gary Craig, founder of EFT (Emotional Freedom Technique); Carol Look, Attracting Abundance through EFT; Bijan of Effortless Prosperity; Anthony Robbins, Unleash the Power Within; Karen Kingston's Space Clearing & Clutter Clearing; Dolores Krieger, PhD, RN, for Therapeutic Touch programs, just to name a few. She is in tune with Abraham-Hicks teachings and the Secret that is centered around the Law of Attraction. She coordinated and held a Bijan/Samia Clearing to Create workshop in Hartford, Connecticut. Sally is also a T. Harv Eker's Millionaire Mind Intensive graduate and a Quantum Leap student and has attended many Peak Potential extensive experiential trainings/courses.

Before her exploration of personal and spiritual development, Sally was an accomplished customer-focused computer professional with over twenty-two years of data processing experience, including twelve years of management and four years of information technologies portfolio management experience with primary emphasis in client/server, distributed computing and midrange technologies. Connect with Sally at www.YourEndlessPossibilities.com.

Nicole Mason, Esq.

FINDING TRUE NORTH

"Where do you really want to be and what do you really want to have in five or ten years and what path will you take?"

The realization that my life had not moved ahead in a decade hit me at probably one of the most opportune times: shortly after I had discovered the world of coaching and Landmark Education. I was sitting in a room full of people wanting to learn how to improve their lives and, as the course continued around me, I found myself contemplating that question—that same one you are always asked during personal development courses, at interviews and on dates: "Where do you want to be in five or ten years?"

When I thought about the question that day, I realized my life fell short of what I had planned and expected for my thirties: basically, a mirror of the show *Thirtysomething*, in which everyone in the group of friends was happily married with kids, living full lives in beautiful homes. At some point I took a wrong turn, got distracted and ran off track. As a result, I did not get what I wanted.

I thought, *Nothing about my life at thirty-six is actually much different from ten years ago. Yes, I have more money and experiences under my belt and I've moved up the corporate ladder, but I've watched most of my friends marry and have kids while also advancing their careers, doing cool things and growing their wealth.*

If they can do it, why can't I? The realization hit me like a ton of bricks, leaving me frustrated and deeply sad.

As I returned home that night, I thought, *I'm still in the same house. Still single. No kids. I have more things now than I did ten years ago, but whom do I have to share them with? What have I really done with all the time that has passed?*

For a while, I thought I had it all. I thought my life was good, being financially comfortable, having an advancing career and what seemed like a full personal life: fun hobbies, good health, personal growth, romantic relationships and friends. But I started to wonder, *Am I on the right track to fulfill all my dreams? Why does something feel missing? What is holding me back? Can I have a great life? Surely, that's possible.*

I'd always practiced the philosophy: "Work to live, don't live to work." I almost never worked on weekends and never worked eighty hour weeks. My way of having a happy, balanced life did not include a family, but eventually the outdoor adventures and travels that used to fulfill and energize me no longer felt enjoyable. On the contrary, they began to make me feel lonely. I found myself feeling empty and uninspired doing the activities I loved and my job was just a job—I had no passion for it anymore. I was in a rut

---

You're burned out, and you've lost your direction.

---

and falling into a depression. Without realizing it, I was living in a way that didn't align with my values.

No matter where I went—be it Asia, South America or Europe—when I would see and hear couples laughing together and sharing their experiences, I ached and longed to find my own life partner. I looked at kids with their parents and thought about which parent they looked like.

Planning my next mountain climb or scuba adventure trip became meaningless; going to restaurants, events and dates on weeknights to "get out there" was tiring; organizing schedules with different friends to ski, hike or do whatever seemed interesting on weekends got tedious. I was constantly spinning my wheels and not really getting anywhere.

It hit me all at once as I stepped through the door to my house that night. Dazed, I sat down on the couch and took stock of my life. At the time, I was a director of government relations and regulatory affairs, traveling between the Bay Area and Los Angeles every week for work. I excelled at my job and had a great reputation in the industry, but I thought I'd hit the glass ceiling.

My personal life was crumbling: I had exited yet another failed relationship with yet another emotionally unavailable man—the only kind of guy I attracted, because I was unavailable for a healthy,

---

I need time to think and recharge.

---

close relationship—and my friendships were eroding, because I was never around. I was stressed, and all the activities I used to do for fun seemed like chores, because I did not have enough energy to give them.

You're burned out, and you've lost your direction. You've gotta reconnect with what really matters and make some big changes, Nicole.

As I sat on my couch assessing my life, it seemed as though I was being hit all at once with every conversation I'd ever had on the subject of family and children. I kept coming back to one in particular, with my friend Theresa. She had chosen to stop working when her children were babies, wanting quality time with her kids and thinking she could go back anytime.

A few years later, at least a year after she had started looking for a job in her profession, she confided in me, "They keep telling me that everything has changed too much, that I'm basically irrelevant because I've been out of the corporate world for a couple of years. If I'd known then what I know now I wouldn't give up my kids for the world, but I miss having a career and if I could do it over, I would do things differently, though I'm not sure how."

By the time I went to bed I was resolved: *I have to reassess my life and my priorities and come up with a new plan, because what I have been doing isn't working to get what I want; I have to make changes and I need a sabbatical to come up with a roadmap.*

"I need some time off. I'm burned out and I need time to think and recharge," I told my employer the next Monday morning with my heart in my throat. Doubts raced in my mind: *What will my employer do while I'm gone? Will my job still be waiting for me in three months?* But I knew in my heart that it was what I needed to do if I would ever have it all, especially what mattered to me most. For once, I made a heart-centered choice instead of a purely practical head-centered one. My heart said, *It doesn't have to be this way. It could be better, it could be great. I can have what I want.*

During that three month leave, I did philanthropic work, got relationship coaching and accepted a new job, for more money and a higher position, with a multi-national company—the only job I interviewed for and only because somebody recommended it to me. I went into my new job as lead attorney, laying groundwork for the flexibility to create space in my life for what I wanted—a healthy, loving relationship—while also growing professionally, proving myself an excellent addition to the company's executive team. I set expectations with everyone in my life in order to support my dream of having a family.

You can't make the same mistakes again You know what you want, and you know that you can have it—you've seen other people do it—so stay focused on it and ask for what you need. I remained committed to my vision of having a career and a full and fun life with a husband who would be my best forever friend with benefits, despite the odds and all circumstances—including fantastically horrid dates that could turn anyone off from dating and the opinions of some who thought I was being unrealistic.

When I did find the right guy, everything flowed naturally and happened fast. I became pregnant at forty-one, immediately after getting married. The entire time I was pregnant, I worried about everything: my career, the baby's health, my health, my husband's readiness to be a dad, my ability to be a mom, finances. Kicking around in my head were thoughts like, *I'm afraid I'm going to lose myself. How are people going to perceive me now, when they've always known me as my career and my adventures? What will my employer do when he finds out that I'm pregnant?* I was losing sight of the big picture and was tempted to think in the short term and just grasp at easy options.

My husband, Anuj, helped me stay focused on the future and our goals during the later stage of my pregnancy. He was in career transition at the time; I helped him negotiate more flexibility and a bigger raise in his new job. His upbringing taught him not to make waves—but he did it anyway for me and our child, securing more

---

"Where do I really want to be in five or ten years?"

---

money, the ability to work from home one day a week and a week's paternity leave. Anuj is so much happier now, and every day that he works from home, he tells me, "Thank you."

While helping him, I realized that I wasn't the only one who had thought, *I can't ask for everything I want; I have to go with the flow.* The truth is, there are always choices and options. It takes courage, but when you look inside yourself to make heart-centered choices that align your day-to-day life with the things that matter most to you, you eliminate distractions and energy drains and access enormous strength and sharp clarity. Imagine enjoying your work, spending time with people you love and respect and having enough money to do all the things that fulfill you. Then ask yourself, "Is it worth being temporarily uncomfortable or scared in order to become permanently fulfilled and happy?"

I did that after I gave birth to my son, when I had to make tough decisions about which direction to go, balancing parenting and work. Drawing from the personal development courses I had taken as well as the coaching training I received and now utilize as a business growth advisor, I realized it was time to reassess my daily actions: was I being inconsistent with any of my most deeply held values?

I compiled a comprehensive, objective list of values that named motivations behind people's actions, like security, independence, intellectual challenge, time with family. Then I took a deep breath, got honest about myself and ranked each on a one-to-five scale to identify what really mattered to me. Values ranked five were critical to reflect and practice in my life. The priority of some core values had shifted over time; it became clear that some things in my life were running against my most critical beliefs and needs.

This values assessment put the spotlight on what in my life was getting in my way, and shed light on the path forward to get where I wanted to be in the future.

Becoming aware of what's creating your current situation does take some time—the biggest challenge can be finding time to assess your own values and how they track, or don't, with the way you are living. Ask yourself, "If I treated myself like a client or my own child, what would I do differently? What am I willing to make non-negotiable?"

I reminded myself that I had choices—I was not at the mercy of circumstance. The values assessment tool I created and now share with others helped me realign with my true North and surround myself with support, so much so that I felt secure enough to start the business I had been planning for six years. It wasn't easy and it didn't seem like the perfect time, but it was the right time. It was a heart-centered and thoughtful choice aligned with my values and vision of my future. Know what you want and persistently stay the course toward what is most important to you—your true north.

My typical day now is a lot different from that unchanging decade. Now, every evening I'm greeted by my son running to me with squeals of joy and love and a warm hug from my husband. I never feel lonely; my husband and I share the highs and lows of our days with each other. I'm doing work that makes a difference in the world and that I love doing. I still travel and do things outdoors; now I get to share that with my son as well as my husband. At fortysomething, my life looks like that *Thirtysomething* dream I had abandoned somewhere along the way. My life is almost unrecognizable from what it was just two years ago and is headed in the direction I want to go.

"Where do you see yourself in five or ten years?" is the question you will be asked or may ask yourself. But instead, try asking, "Where do I really want to be in five or ten years?" Then challenge yourself, "Is that really where I want to be, or just where I assume I will be?" Assess your life and values, discover your true north, and you will gain clarity to make decisions that will move you toward your goals and dreams.

Nicole Mason, Esq., is a licensed attorney, bestselling author, professional speaker, trainer and former corporate executive with over seventeen years' experience working in a variety of business and legal roles. Nicole now helps entrepreneurs and established business owners increase profitability and improve business operations by identifying and implementing strategic changes. Her company, Omnivantage Business Professionals Inc., provides business growth consulting and change facilitation services as well as professional continuing education courses (for CLE, CPE and CE credits) to licensed professionals. Nicole wrote the forthcoming book, Inspired Performance, Successful Employee Engagement in the Age of the Millennial. *Her insightful, proven systems and methods help people get more clients and revenue in their businesses while improving the quality of their lives. Start your own journey toward having it all at www.PeakPerficiency.com.*

Irene Aldrich

REVITALIZING JOURNEY

Standing in front of the mirror, I felt a sense of apprehension. I had always felt a split second of fear about what I would see in it: scars or bruises, or even just the sadness in my own eyes from a lifetime of stress and abuse. I'd spent a lifetime internalizing the toxicity of the environments around me—toxic words, toxic actions, toxic energy. I absorbed all of these toxins, and they made themselves known on my skin, on my heart, on my soul.

Today, though, my reflection showed me just how far I'd come from the scared young girl I once was. A confident woman looked back at me, clear-skinned and strong, happy, fit and healthy. I was smiling.

A feeling of accomplishment swept through me like a wave. *I* had done this. *I* had achieved this. Through my own determination to never give up, my own resolve to know myself and my own drive to heal myself, I was now a self-assured, powerful being. My heart, my mind and my body all hummed with a wellness frequency, each part in perfect balance with the others.

I just never gave up.

From the time I was twelve years old, I had a terribly painful skin condition that caused me great anxiety and stress. I was teased about it, harassed about it. I hid my face; I wore only the baggiest of clothes. I hid myself away.

This problem was brought on by a myriad of causes—not just the inescapable hormones of teenage years, but the bullying and abuse from my family and the people around me. All were detrimental things that just buried my soul. My self-esteem, my self-confidence and my health all suffered from the damaging words and actions of the very people who were supposed to support me. I left home at an early age, trying to evade the stress and the constant unease there. I ran into marriage at a very young age, escaping one abusive relationship only to find one much worse. I survived seventeen and a half years in that marriage; I lived in constant fear for my life, every single day. My conditions, my soul, my energy all deteriorated even further.

What really pushed me to further my journey, to reclaim my own balance, was seeing my four children begin to be hurt by that relationship. I swore those kids were not going to go through the same things I had, growing up. I swore I was not going to lose those kids.

I jumped into healing my own body. I went through a separation and divorce and that got rid of a lot of stress and abuse. And after that, I could focus on my children and myself and settle my mind, settle my soul and work on my body. I could focus more on

I was now a self-assured, powerful being.

nutrition, be with my children and feel the energy of the earth. It took about another eleven months until my skin condition cleared up, after years of chronic recurrence.

I read, studied and researched everything I could find about self-healing and wholistic and holistic wellness. Wholistic wellness encompasses the soul-mind-body connection of life. Holistic wellness encompasses the homeopathic, naturopathic and chiropractic systems of therapeutics. Both practices are essential to maintain a balanced life.

Once that healing occurred, I was transformed. My confidence came back. My energy came back. My excitement for life came back. I was a single parent with four children, but I went back to college, full-time, and pursued a computer science degree. And I accomplished that.

I had achieved a state of balance I had not known before. I had much more confidence in myself. I was slim; my body was firm. I was in great shape. I worked out daily. I followed all my natural nutritional routines, all the time. I was driven. And I was scheduled. It just flowed. And it was beautiful. It was a wonderful time for us.

Be persistent in understanding the flow of your own natural frequency. Our spirit is the force within us that gives our bodies life, energy and power. It is the essence of our being in its purest

> *Be persistent in understanding the*
> *flow of your own natural frequency.*

and most concentrated form. Our natural frequency is that place where we comfortably reside, vibrate and flow, like a pendulum in motion, without resistance.

The advantage of understanding our individual, natural frequency is the comfort we experience in knowing our natural path. It provides us with a foundation with which to integrate our wholistic life. It is essential for us to pay attention to this frequency, as it is an invisible thread to which everything links. It weaves beyond our wholistic and holistic self to our relationships, our environment and our success.

The many energy connections within you affect your alignment and how your mind and body works. When you respect those connections, and use holistic principles, you will see and feel your progress. It is essential to have good nutrition, not just for your body, but for your mind and soul as well. The best type of nutrition differs from one person to another. Not everything will work in the same way for one person as it does for another.

You need to be patient and allow appropriate time before you will notice your progress. If it's not working, add something else to the picture, or take something away. Change something. You have to be willing to learn about yourself, who you are and how *your* body works. It's *your* body, no one else's.

Discover where you feel harmony and peace. This place is that invisible thread, that natural frequency that links to everything. If this is damaged or broken, you may feel resistance and struggle as you are working hard. Recognize when you feel energized.

This is when that invisible thread is no longer damaged or broken. It is now whole and you allow it to become visible. You naturally hum with energy and excitement. You absolutely *love*

It's a continual evolution–there is no endpoint.

---

what you are doing, are having far more fun than you've ever had and never feel as though you are "working." When you are in this space, people around you may comment on your radiance, glow or the vibrant energy that surrounds you.

It's a continual evolution–there is no endpoint. When strain and tension overtake one aspect of our lives, the other aspects are automatically changed as well. If you don't take precautions to recognize and plan ahead when you find yourself in stress, you will find yourself out of balance. You can get lost again.

That is where I found myself one day. Stresses in my personal life caused me to fall off-balance. Another skin condition reared its ugly head. I was lost.

But then I woke up one morning, determined to find my balance again. *No more,* I thought. *I've had enough of this. No more living in these holes. Those people, those energies—they don't get any more of my life.*

Instead of hiding my skin condition, I accepted it. I refused to hide. I could remember how it felt to be in balance and I knew I had the path to get there. I got my nutrition back in line. I focused on getting my body healthy again. And as I started to improve physically, my mind improved as well. I worked on my spiritual and personal development. Rather than hide away from the world, I put myself out in it.

Sometimes the very thing we want to heal, we want to hide. But great power comes in owning it while you're healing it. Great power comes in letting it be part of you, rather than pretending it doesn't exist and waiting for the day it is gone. Accept it as a part of you, instead of letting it define you.

Irene Aldrich is an entrepreneur, lifestyle consultant and founder of Revitalizing Journey, a consciously heart-centered business focused on empowering others and equipping them with the best resources and information to enable them to align, expand and shift the paradigm of their lives.

Having studied and researched wholistic and holistic wellness principles for more than thirty years, Irene leverages her knowledge and experience to help others discover and understand the flow of their own natural frequency and access their truth. Revitalizing Journey provides people with the foundation from which they can integrate both wholistic and holistic principles and create a vibrant, energetic self. Connect with Irene and sign up for a free report at www. RevitalizingJourney.com.

Dagmar Schult

BEYOND LIMITS

I'm flying. Adrenaline is pumping through my veins; I can feel the music flowing through my every cell and all of my concentration is focused. What I'm doing must look effortless but, though I know every last move of this routine, a little inattention could cost us the championship and get me seriously hurt. I flip, I turn; I fly, and my nerves are always on the edge.

Though I'd always been a couch potato as a kid, never doing any sports, when I got to university and started rock 'n' roll dancing, it was like suddenly discovering what my body was always meant to do. I was studying computer science. Students could join various extracurricular sport clubs on the campus, including a rock 'n' roll dance club. I'd liked going out dancing during my later school years and, when I saw the troupe of rock 'n' roll dancers at one of their shows, I thought, *That's so cool. That looks like a lot of fun. I want to do that.*

Rock 'n' roll acrobatics is more a sport than a dance. The women, in particular, are always doing somersaults and flying through the air. Though I was excited to get started, I'd already decided before my first session that I would not do somersaults—it was all scary and there was no way I had the talent to pull it off! Then I started and, in my first lesson, we did some very easy acrobatics that started to build my confidence. Within my first year, I'd progressed so far that I was able to participate in a formation that had won the world championship many times before. Surprisingly, I had a talent for acrobatics.

Rock 'n' roll acrobatics is an incredibly challenging style of dance; you really have to put away your fears. It always felt incredibly exciting—particularly when I mastered moves that I'd been afraid of before. The group had a real sense of camaraderie, lots of social interaction, and the team spirit was what kept me going for the entire twelve years I was doing it—along with the feeling of doing something really special, something extraordinary that others wouldn't dream of doing. I loved the thrill and, of course, the attention; I reveled in the admiration we received from audiences and friends!

It was a great time for me, but not for my body. My body wasn't prepared for the demands I put on it so I had a lot of injuries and a lot of back pain. When you do a sport in a group, you have to function like a robot. If you cannot do it, you are out of the game. So I simply took pain relievers and continued doing what I did, although I knew that it wasn't good for me. I didn't care—everything was so exciting and my goal was to be a world champion. I sacrificed everything for that—even my health.

I experienced pain with every single movement.

When my partner quit dancing competitions, he asked, "Will you keep dancing with me just for fun?"

But at that time, the pain was simply too excruciating to bear any longer, so I told him, "No. I'm in too much pain to enjoy dancing just for the sake of it. When I have less pain, we can give it a chance again."

It was difficult to not dance at first. I'd danced for twelve years, after all; besides working, there was nothing else. Rock 'n' roll had taken up all my free time and I had hardly any friends outside of it—it was my entire world. But I stopped everything, not just the dancing—even as a spectator I no longer went to competitions.

166

Before, my life was rock 'n' roll, and suddenly there was nothing from one day to the next. The only way I could get through it was the hard cut: getting rid of everything.

I experienced pain with every single movement: When I walked, sat down or stood still. I visited doctors, osteopaths and physiotherapists. Nothing helped in the long term and I stopped enjoying doing all the things I loved to do, even going out with people and having fun, because the pain would never leave me. And I had the impression that people started enjoying my company less, because I was not the fun person I used to be.

Much of the time, I was frustrated—unhappy about my life, unhappy about myself and furious at the universe, because it

---

Gratitude is integral to healing.

---

left me alone. *My body isn't working for me. Will I have this pain forever? I don't want it to be this way, but what can I do? I can't find my way out and I can't do anything about it.*

Then I found Rolfing® and, even after a single session, I was pain-free—for a while, at least. It impressed me so much that I decided to become a Rolfer myself. Rolfing® and yoga helped me to restrain the pain, though it never left me completely. My body, especially my back, felt incredibly tense and every once in a while when I made a wrong movement, the pain was there again. *Will all this suffering ever stop?* I thought bitterly.

One night in summer 2011, the pain got so bad that I was afraid I would have to call the emergency doctor. I felt excruciating pain, even though previous X-rays and MRIs had shown only my old rock 'n' roll injuries. It was a dramatic night; I tossed and turned, tears slipping from my eyes at the agony of each movement. *Why me? Why does this have to be so bad? How can living be worth it if it's made of pain? I move like an old woman! I'll never be attractive again. I hate it. This is no life. I cannot stand this anymore.*

And suddenly, as if I were looking down on myself from above, it hit me: *I'm lying here acting like the poor victim, but I'm not a victim. I know that we all create our own lives, so I created all this by myself!*

As soon as I had that thought, it was brilliantly clear—but I had no clue what I could do next. "Okay," I said, comforted by the knowledge even though my teeth were still gritted against the pain, "Okay, I'm a creator, but I'm helpless here. I don't know where to start—I want to live my highest potential, but I need a body that will allow me to do so. And I really need help." Finally, after sending out my plea to the universe, I was able to fall asleep.

Do whatever makes sense in the moment, even if it seems crazy!

When I woke up in the morning with a bit of relief, it was like a little miracle. *Had the universe listened to me?* I'd never prayed or asked or sent out energy before and suddenly I was full of so much gratitude—the universe had answered my prayer and given me some respite. Starting that morning, I made it a habit to thank the universe every evening before falling asleep and every morning when I woke up again—and my back pain got better and better, although I did not change anything else in the beginning. Even in the first few days, I thought, *I might actually have found a solution.*

Then, with a little new hope, I went to my yoga studio where they have a so-called gentle class for the elderly and the yoga teacher showed me some *asanas* (yoga postures) that help mobilize the spine. Even more importantly, he taught me how to breathe properly and do the *asanas* with awareness of what was happening in my body. I started to do yoga at home for about fifteen minutes every day. Soon I realized that, not only was the pain becoming more manageable, I was beginning to feel my bodily sensations again. The healing process took six to nine months.

When rock 'n' roll dancing, I had been like a robot, pushing aside my own thoughts and feelings in order to focus and better serve the group dynamic. I hadn't thought about whether it was good for me or my body or about what I sacrificed. I think part of the reason I had so much pain in my life for so long was that I hadn't been able to feel anything but pain. Finally, I got rid of my back pain and I knew that this was different than before. No longer did I have the feeling that one wrong movement could bring the pain back. It really felt like healing!

Gratitude is integral to healing. We are all energy and, if we have pain somewhere, our energy is blocked. Gratitude and love are energy and bringing the positives into your body makes a difference. Before my healing journey, I wasn't conscious of these things. If you'd asked me then, I would have said, "Yes, of course I am aware of that!" But I don't think I really was. Now, however, I still thank the universe every morning and every night and welcome in the positives.

Instead of letting yourself be a victim, you have to give the idea that you can do something a chance—even when you don't have the first step laid out in front of you. Do whatever makes sense in the moment, even if it seems crazy! Since I had never prayed before, the idea of asking the universe for help was insane to me— but it was the only thing that made sense in that moment. Focus on those things that you're grateful for and, if you take that first step and ask, the universe will jump in and bring solutions to you—it will always give you more of the things you are focusing on.

These days, I'm a live wire. When I was finally able to dance again—not rock 'n' roll this time, but salsa instead—it was a moment of pure elation. I thought, *I have my life back. Here, I can express my feelings: salsa is all about passion, really sensual. I'm finally in the present and connected to my body; I'm not worrying about championship titles or the next competition. I'm flying again; I am in heaven; I am flirting through dance, open to my partner and open for the next move. I'm having fun—I'm happy!*

If you realized the power you have as a creator of your own life, what moments of happiness could you achieve?

Dagmar Schult is an IT professional, a certified Rolfer and runs her own part-time Rolfing® practice to help those afflicted with severe and chronic back pain. To learn more about embracing and being your own creator, connect with Dagmar at www.DagmarSchult.com.

Lane L. Cobb

Let's Dance

Oh my God, I'm fifty, I thought. *What the hell's happened to my life, and what have I done with it? All these years I've believed that taking care of other people is the secret to happiness, that I could pursue my real dreams later. What about me? And how did it get so late?*

An award-winning personal trainer and wellness consultant, I built my life around making sure that everyone in my life—clients, friends, family—was happy, healthy and nurtured. It wasn't just a job; it was a way of life. I told myself it didn't matter that I wasn't fulfilled: *I am "Superwoman," after all. Saving people is what I do.* Even as a child, I was the one people came to when they had a problem. Now, at fifty, I had to come to terms with the fact that there was no later. *Later is now, and I'm the one who needs saving.*

The wake-up call came when I got Lyme disease and had to close my business. As the disease began to affect my ability to think clearly, I could no longer keep track of the details of other people's lives. Nor could I manage the intense physical regimen that kept my body lean, strong and muscular—the armor with which I had always successfully hidden all traces of self-doubt.

Now, my list of regrets was causing me at least as much pain as the disease. Illness forced me to be still, be quiet and listen to that small but insistent inner voice that reminded me: *I'm still not happy. I still haven't followed my heart. With all the life I've lived, I still don't believe in myself.* I had to reckon with that. My time was up and I had to make a change. I decided I had to do whatever it took to make sure that the second half of my life would be fully my own. And with that decision, the memories came flooding back, each with its own lesson attached.

Although I am Black, I was bullied by other Black girls throughout my childhood. My skin was too light. I was too smart. And I lived outside the ghetto. They made sure I knew I didn't belong—every day, without fail. Afraid and embarrassed, I didn't tell anyone what I was going through—not my teachers, not my parents and not my friends. So I felt very much alone and misunderstood, always standing apart. *There must be something wrong with me. Otherwise, why would these girls be so mean to me?* The bullying lasted from elementary school well into high school and I began to believe that I was fatally flawed, unlovable and completely incapable of standing up for myself.

Thinking it must somehow be my fault, but not having any idea why or how to stop it, I tried to fit in by becoming a "people pleaser." I became sexually promiscuous, started cutting classes and almost failed tenth grade. Over the years, my irresponsible sexual behavior resulted in sexually transmitted diseases, unwanted pregnancies, a sullied reputation and a cycle of self-sabotage and depression, which would last well into my adult years. When I was date-raped in college, I blamed myself—as I blamed myself for all the emotionally abusive relationships in which I found myself over the years. And I always told myself I wasn't good enough to follow my dreams.

When I was young, I wanted to be a dancer. Dancing was the joy of my life—the movement, flow and energy of dance filled me with utter bliss. But there was always the question: *Am I doing this right?* In college, I was a principal dancer with the resident dance company. Looking back now, I know how good I was. But at the time, I didn't believe I had what it took to achieve my dream of being a professional dancer. I was so afraid of failing that I didn't even try. *I'm not good enough. I'm not good enough. I don't belong.* It seemed as though, no matter what I did, that voice in my head always chimed in and cut me off at the knees.

When I left college, I stopped dancing. I graduated with a liberal arts degree, not the dance degree I really wanted, and went to work in a job that was completely beneath my skill level. I never went to graduate school and never became a practicing psychologist—another dream wasted.

For many, many years after that, I couldn't go to a dance performance without having my heart wrenched: *Oh my God, that could have been me up there. I could have done that if I'd only believed in myself.* I was so consumed by regret, shame and

> **And I always told myself I wasn't good enough to follow my dreams.**

embarrassment over having sold out on my dreams that I couldn't even enjoy watching what had once brought me so much joy. Instead, I compensated by taking on other activities. Being a fitness instructor at least gave me a chance to move, perform and choreograph, even if just to help my beloved clients get healthy.

But turning fifty was a game-changer. While I was languishing with Lyme disease, I awoke to just how much of my life I had wasted in doubting myself and holding myself back. My mind was filled with memories of the goals I failed to even form, let alone reach, because I didn't think I would be successful; the opportunities I turned down because I was afraid I would be rejected; the choices I did or didn't make because I could not love myself for who I was and because I could not believe that I was, in fact, enough.

Before, I hadn't fully understood the crippling impact of the baggage I carried from my past and that after all this time I was still holding myself back from pursuing my dreams and really being happy. Equally crippling was my constant negative self-assessment: guilt about having given my power over to fear for so many years; shame about having been less than I could have been;

embarrassment that the person who helped others push past their limits hadn't actually moved forward for most of her adult life.

And then something happened. One by one, I began to consciously release those feelings of shame, regret and resentment. I began to take back my power and in doing so I discovered my purpose! I realized that searching for fulfillment in support of others rather than in support of myself was an act more of fear and self-loathing than of virtue. I had to look within for guidance and reinvent myself.

> **I had to look within for guidance
> and reinvent myself.**

Turning points come when the pain of not living your purpose becomes greater than the desire to be safe, and facing down your demons becomes the river you must cross to get to there. Through all my soul-searching, I believed there must have been a reason for my suffering, which would be revealed to me if I looked with an open mind and a forgiving heart at what life had brought me.

The work with my beloved clients taught me every woman is ashamed of something in her past that she doesn't want anyone to know about. Every woman has the capacity for healing and unconditional love, but most bestow it on others and rarely give it to themselves. When I finally saw that, I knew my purpose was to help women like me love themselves unconditionally and to help create a global shift in how women relate to themselves.

I also knew I had to go first. You can't give what you don't have. I knew that everything I was going to ask other women to do, I had to do: *For me to be a leader in unconditional love, I have to experience and express unconditional love—especially for myself. To help women live joyful and fulfilled lives, I have to live joyfully and in fulfillment. I have to make choices that make me happy and must not be afraid to step out.*

When I coach women now, I always tell them, "We all have shame, we all have regret. You have to let it out, so you can let it go." For your soul to live its purpose, it must be unencumbered by shame, regret, remorse, anger or whatever else you might be holding onto. You've got to release those things. Love yourself and live your life. A cacophony of voices is out there telling you that you're not good enough and you can't have what you want. You don't have to add your own voice to the mix.

We may not want to admit to those lost opportunities and missed goals, which we sacrificed because of self-loathing and self-doubt, but our hearts know. Our souls know. Every one of those self-inflicted wounds is stored in our bodies and, out of shame, we try to beat them back and forget they ever happened. But the noise persists in the background and keeps you from enjoying your life.

*Once your baggage is released, your
path forward becomes clear.*

Then you get to be fifty (or forty, or thirty) and you come face to face with the baggage you're still carrying, the baggage you'll need to get rid of in order to have the life you really want to have.

Our spirits know. We get these intuitive hits in our lifetime: This is who you are. This is what you were born for. This is what is possible. While we're still holding onto our baggage (in whatever form it takes), we are unable to hear the universe saying, "This is it, this is where you're supposed to be." Fear, self-doubt and personal limitation are protective devices constructed by the mind (ego) to keep us safe in times of crisis, but they don't allow us to grow. In other words, the only way to transform your life and take on new habits is to let go of the ones that don't work anymore.

Living a life of joy, freedom and satisfaction takes commitment to something other than personal safety. It takes a commitment to making a difference in the world that is in alignment with the purpose for which you were born—without regret or apology, but with unconditional love for and acceptance of yourself and with gratitude for having been given the opportunity to live one more day in the service of that purpose.

Now that I know who I am and what I am here for, I know that wherever I am, I belong. I don't have to wait for an invitation. I'm okay with taking care of me first and everybody else second. And that's a miracle. The most incredibly awesome thing is that, once your baggage is released, your path forward becomes clear. The struggling subsides and you can just choose to be happy.

Within months of writing this chapter, I had a notion that I wanted to dance again. Almost instantly my sister called and said, "My daughter is in a dance performance. We'd really love for you to come. I always tell her about your dancing. And oh, by the way, master dance classes are being given at the college here and I will treat you to the classes if you're interested."

I'm sharing this with you to illustrate the power of choosing your life. Once you choose to live a transformed life, you will hear the voice of your spirit calling you to act. All you have to do is ask for what you want and it will come. You just have to let it in.

I know, all too well, the pain and crippling effect of the self-suppression, self-limitation and self-loathing women allow to keep them from expressing their gifts in the world. But I believe that, if the world is to heal from hatred, poverty, illness and blight, we women must return ourselves to our rightful place in the world: a place of leadership and authority. We always have been—and still are—a force to be reckoned with. We are the healers, the caretakers and the sources of life, universal wisdom and unconditional love. We just have to embrace who we are and believe, once and for all, that we are "enough."

Whether you know it or not, you are already a leader. And when you transform your relationship with yourself from one of limitation to one of empowerment and authenticity, your purpose will reveal itself and you can embrace it without apology or regret. Sit down with yourself and take a look. Decide to love yourself. Listen to your heart. Release your shame and celebrate your singular life. You are more than worthy and more than good enough. Your spirit is calling. Let's dance!

Lane Cobb is a speaker, transformational author and holistic intuitive life coach committed to helping women create more joy, freedom, prosperity and authenticity in life. Her passion is empowering women to tell the truth about who they are and what they want so they can live their purpose and fulfill their rightful destiny. Creator of the "Intuitive Body Coaching Method," Lane helps women connect with their spirituality and honor themselves and their bodies as unique, gifted, intuitive and powerful beyond their own imagining.

Lane is nationally certified in many coaching and healing modalities and has helped hundreds of women to live their highest purpose and achieve their greatest potential. She is also the author of Be Your Biggest Champion—A Self-Esteem Guide for Teen Girls *(Xulon Press, 2014). Connect with Lane at www.LaneCobb.com.*

Carol Smith

SUCCEEDING IN FORGIVENESS

"Congratulations, Carol," my gynecologist declared, "you're pregnant."

I was stunned. I stammered a reply, and hung up the phone. *Me? Pregnant? This couldn't be happening. Unwed girls from my small town didn't get pregnant. I can't be pregnant. What will the neighbors think? What about my plans for college, for a career, for a wedding?* Sure, I was physically attracted to my high school boyfriend, but neither of us was ready for marriage. It can't be true! *I don't want to be pregnant!*

In 1974, abortion had just been legalized but it was never discussed. The name of a clinic was given to me, a clinic that would make such mistakes go away. During those next few days I moved through a state of emotional numbness and then I did away with the one thing that stood between me and my future plans.

That decision haunted me for decades. I told very few people; most of my friends and relatives never knew. I hid my choice deep in my soul. *How could I have made such a decision? What kind of demon had possessed me? What would others think if they knew the truth about me? But, I'm a "good girl."*

The thought of being judged was the driving force that kept my secret safe. It also kept me in pain and suffering.. Resigned now to never have children of my own. That was my punishment. Grieving for years over my empty womb, accepting the life sentence of never being called "Mom." Believing I was unworthy of the title.

Grief overcame me one day while on a flight from Los Angeles to San Francisco. *It's gone,* I thought. *I would never get to experience that pregnancy.* I would not have that child, or any other. *How did I get to this point?* I remember calling out to God through my tears, "God, if you really exist, I need to know you NOW! What will others think of me? If only they knew who I really am."

God's answer came in loud and clear, "Carol, don't worry about what others think. You are my child and, for all eternity, you have been found innocent." Remembering Romans 8:1-2: "Therefore, there is no condemnation for those who know Christ, because through Christ the law of the Spirit who gives life has set you free." I have felt the presence of God ever since.

God offered me forgiveness, but it took a long time for me to accept it. Difficulty came in appreciating its truth—I couldn't believe it included me. I didn't feel worthy. Accepting God's love meant letting go of my guilt. That was a huge challenge. Guilt fueled my self-imposed judgments—I was not worthy of love. I had to protect my heart and hide the key. Guilt, shame and grief influenced my decision-making process. Whenever the topic of

That decision haunted me for decades.

abortion came up, I would cringe. I didn't want to be part of the conversation. I would try to deny that I was in any way connected with that word.

A friend who knew I'd had an abortion once gave my name and number to someone to call and discuss my choice. I was mortified. *How dare you let someone else know? That's my private story, I don't want to talk to anyone about it.*

Several years later, I finished college and had a good career, just as I had planned. My goals were achieved and my story was safely buried. I made sure I didn't get close to anyone, barely dating from the time I was twenty until I was forty. I chastised myself, avoided intimacy that might cause me to reveal my shameful history, and took no chances of ever getting pregnant again. I made sure I went out with a group of people, and didn't allow myself to be separated from the group. Once in a while I would go on a date or two, but that would be it. I didn't allow myself to get too close. All the while, I continued to hide my heartbreak over my desires to be married and have a family. I forbade myself to have those joys because of the overwhelming feelings of guilt and shame. These things are clear to me now. Back then, I wasn't able to connect the dots.

I was just afraid of having an intimate relationship. Pangs of jealousy surged through me when I saw friends and family who were happily married, parenting beautiful children, and living in

---

Guilt fueled my self-imposed judgments.

---

the homes of their dreams. *Where had the years gone? Was I ever going to get past this?*

And then there was this one guy. We had been friends for several years. We ran with the same crowd. We had common interests and even shared a mutual love for scuba diving—all as strictly platonic friends. When he expressed interest in a deeper relationship, I bolted. A year later, a chance encounter brought him back into my life. We even began traveling together! I asked myself questions like: *Why do I like being around this guy? What is it about him that makes him different from the rest? What would it take for me to consider dating him? What would it cost me if I lost him?*

I made my list: he's traveled the world; he's adventurous; he's intelligent; he's unafraid; he's kind and he cares about me. I listed all the wonderful things he did for me. *So, if I admire and like him so much, why am I terrified of going on a date with him?* Eventually, we did go out and I knew I had to tell him about my past. Telling him before we got married was a requirement. *But what if he doesn't want to be with me?* I had to overcome my fear. I had to take the risk. I had to muster the courage to share my most intimate and personal secret. Trusting in our relationship, I felt he would accept my confession with love and care. But it was still very difficult to unlock that part of my life.

I said, "I have to share something with you and if it changes your mind about marrying me, then that's the way it will have to be." I needed to tell him the truth to set myself free. I told him. He didn't change his mind. He made me feel safe and accepted. He took me in his arms and comforted me. I felt cherished. I recall the moment as if it were yesterday.

Six weeks after our first date, he popped the question. As he presented me with an emerald promise ring and asked me to marry him, I said, "To the best of my knowledge." We've been married almost nineteen years now.

We had the big church wedding that I'd always wanted. Though not a virgin, I wore a white wedding gown anyway. The dress made me feel like a princess. Sure, I felt a twinge of guilt at wearing white. But everyone knew I hadn't dated in twenty years; if I wore a different color, eyebrows would be raised. Questions would be asked. So, I enjoyed the beautiful day with friends and family, my story still safe.

There were other things that added to my pile of guilt. I lost my brother to suicide, raising unending questions: *How could I not have known what he was going through? How could I have changed his mind? Did he know how much I loved him?* Several years later, I stood over my mother as she lay in her hospital bed. The doctor advised our family that we should consider discontinuing life support and we reluctantly agreed. As the nurse disconnected my mother and she took her last breath, grief visited me again.

It wasn't until a few years later, during my own trip to the hospital in Detroit, that I took inventory of my life. I was suffering from vertigo, nausea, and yes, tension and stress. That was the day I resolved to find a way out from this burden of shame and guilt. I was guilty of not accepting God's offer of forgiveness. Again, I had so many questions: *What would it take for me to let this go? When would I be ready? What if I was sent to earth to do something seemingly unforgivable, so God could show me what love is? Is there a way for God to find that hidden key to my heart?* The answer to the last one is yes. I believe the key is forgiveness. I read *The Law of Forgiveness* by Connie Domino. It changed my life. I started forgiving everyone and everything I could think of, especially myself. I heard God say, "Innocent. Carol, I am raising your child."

So, I've spent the last couple of years accepting God's forgiveness. One of the instrumental elements of my growth has been Peak Potentials. I've attended many events that have helped strengthen my confidence, courage and ability to love. I've begun to challenge myself. I invested in a real estate opportunity. I even went skydiving!

Forgiven, I feel lighter, more open, more grounded, and more loving of myself. I am more in tune with my environment and what's going on around me. My instincts are heightened and my spiritual awareness more authentic. The act of forgiveness created space for miraculous blessings to come into my life. People from

I believe the key is forgiveness.

my past have called out of the blue. At a class reunion, I saw the man who would have been the father of my child, and after forty years, was able to ask for his forgiveness. Not to mention, I've put my story in print for others to read. Now, that's a miracle!

I see my family through new eyes, without the shadow of shame. My husband is the most wonderful, loving, caring, compassionate, smartest, wittiest man I know. I am blessed everyday by my siblings and their children and their children's children. I am blessed to be able to pour my love into the next generations. Best of all, I am blessed to share my authentic self with everyone. Forgiveness has reconciled my spirit with the spirit of my Creator.

Not forgiving yourself is a huge barrier to success. Not feeling worthy prevents you from doing the work you need to do. When you are offered an opportunity, you might say no or just let it pass you by, because, deep down, you believe you don't deserve it. Your mistake doesn't have to be something like terminating a pregnancy; it could be as simple as making a mistake at work. You don't tell anyone, no one else knows, but as long as you carry the secret guilt of that mistake, are you really going to ask for the raise or try for the promotion?

Lack of forgiveness not only robs you of the healing balm that it provides, but keeps you from the promise of what you can accomplish. To begin the process of forgiving yourself, seek out compassionate healers. Meet with them. Read their writings. Practice their teachings. Set your intentions and then expect miracles. The price of admission is gratitude.

Carol Smith earned her bachelor of science degree in physical therapy. She worked as a physical therapist in California for twenty years. Her nearly forty year struggle with the burden of guilt and the adverse impact it had on her life have motivated her to find ways to help other people who are similarly burdened. She hopes her story has blessed you.

Natasha Cooke

THE REMARKABLE
ENERGY OF INTENTION

What are you doing here? Only YOU can find out...

I was born to a Korean family on remote Sakhalin Island in far-eastern Russia. Following the death of my beloved mother when I was five years old, I grew into young adulthood in an atmosphere of hard work, with no support or understanding.

Given my beginnings, it would have been understandable if I had not survived. I had no guidance, no help, no love, no friends, no safe place, not even enough food sometimes. But, I was blessed: From the start, I had a connection with source. *God is always looking after me.*

I didn't recognize until many years after I escaped my childhood home that my soul emerged filled with great purpose and that my faith in my own destiny had begun to unfold when I was still very young.

One sunny day, sitting at the window of our apartment in the small town of Yuzhno-Sakhalinsk, I looked out at the clear blue sky and warm, caressing rays of the sun and felt complete agony. *I just don't know what to do. I'm so lost.* It was such a beautiful day outside, but there was no joy inside me.

I asked God: *Why do I feel this way? The world is beautiful—this blue sky, green trees all around—life should be a joy! Why am*

I so alone? What is the reason for all this pain and struggle? Life shouldn't be like this. What am I doing here? Why was I born in this place? I was very young, maybe sixteen, but I already knew I couldn't just stay on Sakhalin my whole life and continue living this way, end of story. My whole life I'd been treated as though I was nothing, as though I could do nothing right. But even more strongly than I believed that, I thought, *I want to get off of this ride.*

Talking to God gave me courage. Something truly magical started happening in that moment. When I spoke the words of my intention out loud with clarity: "I'm going to leave this place

---

Why am I so alone?

---

and see what this big world has to offer me. I am going to own an international passport, going to find my people, the ones who will love me and enjoy life. So be it!"

The energy of my own intention was enough to change my circumstances. It propelled me into the world. My goal decided, I took immediate steps to leave. I accepted my first job in a restaurant on Saipan, an island in the Pacific on the other side of the world from Sakhalin, and I never looked back.

Years of travel and adventure ensued. I lived in several different countries, enjoying many cultures and encountering many inspiring people. Eventually, I met my husband and put down roots in Los Angeles.

Life was pretty great. Even though I had hepatitis C, discovered during my first pregnancy, which my doctors said was incurable, I felt healthy. I could do nothing about it, so as long as I felt strong, I pushed it to the back of a busy life. Both of my children were healthy and happy, thank God. We all loved living in sunny California. My husband and I threw ourselves into a new business, creating a chain of retail stores that became quite successful.

And then, things started to fall apart.

When we don't listen to our intuitions, chasing financial goals, life throws us, blind and deaf, into the deepest darkness of our lives and we call it crisis. And that happened to our family. When the market crash came in 2008, business at our retail chain crashed, too. At first, we were forced to lay off employees. Then we started closing stores. A death lawsuit shattered our life. My husband was losing his mind. We couldn't pay the mortgage and our house was sold on short sale.

While all this was going on, my disease really started acting up. I was exhausted all day, every day. I had known for a while that I needed to give significant attention to my own healing—I'd had this problem for years; it must have been taking even more of a toll than I knew. I started to slide into depression.

I knew my heart was closed. But, something in my soul poked at me and said, *This is the time for you to ask for help. You need guidance. You need to find your true path.* I knew I needed

---

None of these paths were my own.

---

something deeper to show me the way out, just as talking to God had freed me from a sad childhood and a bleak future on Sakhalin so long ago.

Again, the energy of intention drove immediate change in my life. It started with caring enough about my health to pursue healing, even though we were in bad financial shape. For months, I tried different spiritual and physical treatments of all kinds. I even saw a psychic. My soul didn't buy it. None of these paths were my own and I could feel it.

My search continued until one day I saw an ad in a Russian newspaper: "Emil Bagirov, Doctor of Science, a physicist, the rector of the Moscow Institute of Cosmoenergy and Psychology and the head of the Cosmoenergy School, is coming to Los Angeles to help you eliminate stress and depression and bring luck and balance into your life." Something spoke to me. *Why not! I'll try it. This is clearly meant to be!*

So I went to the seminar. The method captured my imagination and my soul sang. I learned that everything is connected, everything is based in energy and each kind of energy has a vibration. By changing my vibration, I could change just about anything. This idea appealed to me—again, I was shown that my own intention and the energy of my intention were incredibly powerful.

I began to feel real hope again. Doors of opportunity began to open. The hepatitis C got better and disappeared within six months. My husband and I signed up for a self-improvement seminar together and kept going for years. With our own vibrations raised,

You have infinite universal energy to draw on.

we raised the vibration of our business. And we started to notice, month after month and then year after year, the numbers going up, even though we hadn't made many changes in strategy and it wasn't due to significant economic recovery in our industry. We grew our business into over a million dollars in annual sales. Now it is time to give something back to humanity.

I directly connect all the monumental changes in my life to the changes in my vibration. We become different people as our vibrations are raised and, in every layer of our lives, things begin to transform from difficult and scarce to abundant and overflowing. Changes in my vibration led me to open further to my own spirituality as I had wished; I began traveling again, reading metaphysical books and learning like a new student. I started to grow toward the universal energy source and therefore to my true destiny. Today, I am on my true path as a practitioner and teacher of cosmoenergy.

That higher source is everything. When you work with the higher source, you conduct the power of that source to every patient, student or seeker. It works on the whole body, mind and spirit at once, not just certain problems. Changing your vibration through tapping into this energy helps with health problems, financial problems, behavioral and relationship problems—life changes in every area. We get in touch with spirituality. Situations change. Life feels more expansive and harmonious. The soul finds inner wisdom. You find yourself interacting with the right people in the right situations, choosing *your* path to destiny.

What are you doing here? Do you know? Every soul comes to Earth with the purpose of fulfilling itself. Listen to your intuition and seek out your purpose. When you have a clear vision of that purpose, set goals and stick to them, taking strong actions aligned with your heart. Set goals daily, weekly, monthly and yearly with specific outcomes. Charge them with intentions and emotions. Write them down and stick to them. Make sure all the actions you take toward these goals are aligned with your heart. Discipline, persistence, responsibility, authenticity and spiritual foundations will take you far to reach your purpose.

You have infinite universal energy to draw on in bringing you closer to a joyful and balanced life. In your DNA, you have an ability to fly, walk over water, materialize yourself. Find your freedom! Start by seeking, educating yourself, finding teachers and mentors and peers who hunger for the same light. Learn for yourself and your family to fulfill your destiny in this lifetime.

Almost every person I work with tells me, "I want to find my purpose in this life." Ask yourself: What pain do I carry, especially from childhood? If you think abuse traumatized you, heal yourself first, then help others to heal their souls. If you feel a lack of love from your parents, find compassion and unconditional love in your heart first, then spread it out to the world. Once your desire for change becomes clear, intention, huge desire and a strong connection to the source of universal energy will take you to new heights in no time.

Natasha Cooke is a healer, practitioner and a teacher of cosmoenergy. In Moscow, Natasha studied at E.M. Bagirov's School of CosmoEnergy and PsychoAnalysis and D. Boevodin's school, CosmoEnergy Portal "Unity," and earned her Progressor of Cosmoenergy. She also studied with John Kehoe (Quantum Warrior) and Peak Potentials and with South American shamans in Peru and spent a year with enlightened master Paramahamsa Nithyananda (Inner Awakening, No Food Program) in India. She is a member of the International Classic CosmoEnergy Federation (ICCF), which is in alliance with the World Health Organization. Connect with Natasha at www. CosmoEnergyPortal.com.

Nellie Williams

Chasing Shiny Objects

Countless success stories are built upon the foundation of someone having a single-minded purpose. What you focus on expands until the universe itself seems intent upon delivering what you're working for. You just need to know what you want and keep focusing on it, taking one step after another and not letting anyone or anything discourage you.

That seems easy enough, doesn't it? And yet, so often along the way you will find shiny objects that distract your attention and tempt you into wasting time, money and effort on things that don't bring you much beside hopes. Those shiny objects can come in the form of business ideas, golden opportunities, or seemingly easy sources of additional income; you may be looking for them yourself in order to generate more money or you may just happen upon them by accident.

Whatever the case, don't chase the shiny objects. Don't chase the money. It will elude you.

I'm a former Internal Revenue Service (IRS) auditor and audit supervisor. After five years of working for the government, I left the well-paying, stable job and started my own business, knowing that I wanted to be of service to people. I opened an income tax practice, where I prepare tax returns and represent clients who are being audited by the IRS. I only had one client and dreams of success when I started almost thirty years ago, but I just took that first step and said, "I'm gonna make it work."

And I did. Yes, it was a challenge—part of that was cash flow, part building a client base—but everything worked out. I knew what I wanted to do; I knew there was a market for this kind of personalized, specialized service, even with H&R Block® stores all over the place. I had a different approach. Thanks to my experience, I didn't just prepare my clients' tax returns—I also told them what the IRS was going to see in those tax returns. I was following something that I believed to be of value and my business flourished.

Despite my positive attitude, however, the events in the economy had been dragging me down these last years, affecting many parts of my life, until I started looking into additional ways in which I could bring in money. As a life-long learner who is interested in many things and believes in personal development, I thought expanding into new markets, beyond taxes, might be a good idea.

Trying to chase those elusive shiny things, I invested thousands of dollars in pursuits like learning about real estate. I still have a shelf full of books on the subject, but I never actually pulled the trigger and purchased a property—it seemed like a bigger risk than

> *Don't chase the shiny objects. Don't chase the money. It will elude you.*

I was willing to take, going beyond what I know. I have also tried multi-level marketing and other business opportunities. None of them have panned out. They've been interesting, but they all required a lot of work and brought little financial reward. I spent a lot of time and effort, only to realize that I'm really good at what I do and I shouldn't deviate from what I know because that's where my heart is.

Looking around now, I notice how many people seem to fall into the same traps—chasing money and finding ideas or opportunities that seem great, but aren't really productive or financially beneficial. So often people diversify too much, following different income streams, looking for money instead of doing things they're passionate about. I have clients who work really hard building their businesses and invest a lot of time and money only to be ahead by a few hundred dollars each year. When they come to me after they've chased those shiny objects, they have nothing but expenses to show for it.

One of the reasons people chase shiny objects seems to be their inability to see the full value of what they have to offer.

Your experience, your skill set and interests all add up to something unique. If it's of value and you can monetize it, following your dream and doing what you love will bring you more money

*Your experience, your skill set and interests
all add up to something unique.*

and success than chasing after more elusive things. Life is not one big variety store. You have a lot of things to entertain you, but in the end, you need to think: *What's gonna get me through the day, the week, the month, the year?* And who says you can't enjoy your work? It's okay to love what you do and do what you love.

For me, the greatest boost of confidence came from Mr. Bill Walsh, "America's business developer." When Bill invited me to learn about his Million Dollar Speaker Bootcamp, he said he would evaluate my application. He wanted to know whether or not I had a topic that would appeal to many people. When I worked for the IRS, I learned that nobody wants to talk with the tax auditor. Now that I am "your side" of the IRS, people want my help, but they may not always want the true answers to their tax questions.

When Bill told me he thought I had a valuable topic in "Bulletproof Your Taxes," I said to myself, *Really?* He told me that my work is worth sharing with more people than just the few hundred I see every tax season.

He said, "Spread your message. Teach more people how to avoid any future audits by filing their most accurate tax return, how to take their maximum legal deduction and pay their lowest legal tax."

Mr. Walsh's words were not my first clue that I should focus on what I do best. I already knew that I should not divert my energy switching paths or taking several paths at once, but stay the course, dig deeper and expand within my area of expertise. And I believed that the right path was doing what was real and authentic for me. His encouragement to apply to the speaking bootcamp was just a final confirmation that it was possible. I could affect more people and share my knowledge to help them avoid trouble with the IRS.

I learned from my friend, T. Harv Eker, that your beliefs lead to your thoughts, your thoughts lead to your feelings, your feelings lead to your actions and your actions lead to your results. Every year I help many hundreds of people with their taxes. I have seen how the economy has affected each person differently and I admit that I had strong feelings about what I believed to be

Start by finding out where your heart is.

right. I was disappointed to see that things were not going as I expected or wished for some of these people. I could not see hope of improvement in the short term. Allowing my empathy and negative feelings to override my positive feelings brought me down both in my business and personal life, even though I am normally a happy and positive person .

Your thoughts are like magnets—they will attract. So guard your thoughts. Pay attention to your feelings. Take action. Your outer results are a mirror of your inner beliefs. If you don't like what you see, first ask yourself what thoughts you need to change. And then take the actions that will lead to a new result.

Helping people, knowing that what I do for them is genuine and I'm not taking their money under false pretenses, is what makes me feel good about my job. It's not some kind of dream-in-a-box; it's my authentic passion and my very real expertise. It's sharing what I'm best at. Branching out into speaking to groups and offering my coaching programs to share my knowledge with a wider audience is another avenue within the same business.

My next step is to speak to more groups and build up my coaching practice, so I can train more people in what definitely to include and what to stay away from when filing tax returns. It's a challenge, stepping out of my comfort zone, but that's what makes it important; there's no pot of gold at the end of the rainbow within your comfort zone.

Start by finding out where your heart is. The best job for you is doing what you love and what you're passionate about. If you find it and it's not a pipe dream, but something of value that you can monetize—a profession, not a hobby—don't let anyone talk you out of pursuing it. Don't let anyone steal your dream. Dig deeper and find out how you can expand within your business, but don't waste time and effort chasing shiny objects. It is certainly good to have multiple sources of income, but first, you need to focus and stay the course, taking one step at a time.

Remember, you are in charge of your own attitude, your habits and your future. You have to keep going. Keep learning. Keep growing.

Nellie Williams, enrolled agent, is an author, speaker, trainer, consultant and coach. Her experience working with the Internal Revenue Service as a tax auditor and tax audit supervisor gave her practical knowledge of how the IRS works and thinks. Nellie uses her insider knowledge to help individuals and small business owners understand the rules of the tax game. Her coaching programs arm her clients with knowledge they can use for the rest of their taxpaying lives to stay out of the jaws of the IRS. She can help you meet your own personal money archetype and understand what motivates you and what challenges you about money. She helps her clients pay their lowest legal tax. But she wants you to have to pay a lot of tax, because that means you will have made a LOT of money. Connect with Nellie at www.BulletproofYourTaxes. com.

Latonya Collins

STEP OUT OF THE BOX

After yet another failed conversation with my teenaged daughter, Tamara, which ended with a bedroom door being closed and a barrier effectively put between us, I sat down at my kitchen table and sighed. Bills surrounded me. I started to work through them methodically, prioritizing and figuring out how I would shift money around this month.

As I worked through the bills, I zoned out—I'd been doing it so long, it was second nature—and my thoughts strayed back to Tamara. She'd been listless and morose lately, and her grades had been slipping. I'd tried to talk to her about it, but our conversations never seemed to get off the ground. *When did she start acting like this?* I wondered. *Did something happen to her that she can't tell me about? Why wouldn't she come and talk to me if something was really wrong?*

Bills now forgotten, I racked my brain; but try as I might, I couldn't pinpoint even a small shift in her behavior that might indicate a reason for why she was so low. It all seemed so familiar, though. And then I realized why: it was history repeating itself.

During my childhood and teens, my mother had to work a lot to support my siblings and me and was away from us most of the time. My mother, my grandmother and my aunties were all single parents—it seemed to be an unbreakable cycle in our family—

and I grew up in what really amounted to a no-parent household. Mom was always working two or three jobs to put food on the table and we always had the material things we needed; yet I still found myself starving to death from a lack of love and affection. Her presence was what I longed for the most.

The hunger for that love and presence had me on a self-destructive path, where I would seek love and attention from people who lacked love themselves, always attracting those who would verify the feelings I already had about myself: shame, self-hatred and overwhelming sadness.

It only got worse when I became pregnant at fifteen. I had a lot of people who looked down on me, at school and at the hospital, but no one to ask, "What's going on inside you that you ended up like this?"

I didn't have anyone around to tell me that what I was doing was wrong; some parents set rules about what you shouldn't do and you do it anyway, but I had no rules. I simply followed the crowd, not understanding how I got to this place where nobody was willing to talk to me about it but would still say negative things about me being pregnant.

I sank into an even deeper state of depression and, though being a mother made me grow up pretty fast, I was still a child. I still didn't know how to process and deal with the feelings of shame and despair that plagued me—not in a healthy way, at least. I attempted suicide many times, but only succeeded in waking up in a hospital, getting my stomach pumped. Each time, I tried the counseling offered, hoping in vain that it would help, but it never did. Talking about the problem didn't make it go away, because it didn't change the fact that I was completely love-starved.

My life became a cycle of doing what needed to be done in order to support myself and Tamara. Eventually, I married and had a son and things got better—until I became pregnant with my third child. My husband and I both lost our jobs within weeks of one another and it wasn't long before we were behind on our mortgage and bills.

When I was seven months along, my husband told me that he loved and wanted to be with someone else.

Back to square one, I thought after he left, wandering numbly around my home in the days following the foreclosure notice. *What am I going to do now?*

My first priority was finding a place to stay; I found myself on my way to the homeless shelter. When I got there, however, my feelings of shame and guilt were too much for me to deal with, so much so that all I wanted was to be alone with my kids. We slept in the car that night, under the car porch of our foreclosed home.

The stress and depression that broke over me like a wave caused me to go into early labor, leaving me with two kids to take care

---

Her presence was what I longed for the most.

---

of and a third in the hospital on a breathing machine. A week afterward, desperate for a suitable place for my three children to live, I went to a temp agency.

"I'll do anything," I told them, trying to keep my face as bright as possible—I couldn't let them see that, inside, I was breaking.

I told no one that I'd given birth only a week before. And though my body was a wreck, I started working in a car plant, picking up heavy car parts. Not letting myself cry out as pain shot through my body was an exercise in self-control and I spun further into depression, struggling with overwhelming loneliness. I had no one to talk to or ask for help.

When I finally got an apartment, I thought things would get better. *Now things have to start looking up,* I thought, after we got settled in with the few possessions we had left. *Now we're all going to be okay.* But did you ever hear that phrase, "Don't speak too soon?" I'd *thought* too soon—after paying the bills, I found myself unable to buy diapers for my son. All the resolve and hope I'd had when we moved in crumbled away as if it had never been there in the first place. What sort of a useless mother was I, that I couldn't even provide the basic necessities for my babies?

It seemed I had only one option left. Pills didn't work—I'd tried that already. I dropped the kids off at daycare—but instead of going to buy a gun with the money from my next small paycheck as I'd planned, I went back to my apartment and broke down utterly.

Crying and crying, I asked God, "Please help me, deliver me from my mind. I don't understand the fight that's going on inside me and I just want some help."

I cried myself out in that apartment, feeling no less helpless afterward, but at least believing I could still pick myself up and

---

I had no one to talk to or ask for help.

---

carry on—my babies needed me. They were counting on me to take care of them and provide them with what they needed to live.

All of these memories surged through my mind like a wave as I sat at the kitchen table—for years now, I'd been following the same pattern as all the mothers in my family: working multiple jobs to support my kids, never being at home to show them love or give them what they needed, and now my daughter was displaying the same behaviors that I had in my teens.

I was doing exactly what I'd sworn I never wanted to do. *There has to be another way. I want more for my kids than for them to grow up with shame and depression. I have to break this cycle once and for all.*

I made the decision to stop following these destructive patterns that were not serving me. And though I knew that creating better habits would be a long process, I was up for the challenge—the box that was familiar to me was no longer useful and I had to get out. My kids needed to see their mommy happier, healthier, more successful and making consistent efforts to love herself and them as much as possible.

Loneliness still plagued me. I had no one to really talk to about it. But I wrote in my journal and prayed and put aside much more time to focus on solutions rather than on what I was going through. I was able to repair my credit and purchase a new home—something I thought I would never be able to do again—and I started seeking career choices that would enable me to work from home and be more flexible, ways that I could have income to support my kids but still be there as a mother, as a whole person.

We tend to cling to what we know, even if what we know is horrible. There's comfort in what's familiar and we stay inside the box because we don't know what's outside. *But what's outside the box* must *be better than this,* I thought over and over, repeating it to myself like a mantra. It fueled me finding an opportunity to work from home and suddenly I had hope again. My first day working from home, I was smiling but jittery, worrying about whether I would have enough discipline to do the work without

The box that was familiar to me was no longer useful and I had to get out.

any guidance. But I'd always had to be hardworking, so I knuckled down and accomplished what needed to be done—months went by this way. It really was the best choice I ever made.

Looking back at how much shame and self-hatred I once had—as opposed the way I love myself and my life now—is amazing. I used to focus so much on the storm, on the challenge, that I lost focus on myself, on my dreams, passions and goals, and on motherhood. I'm a living witness to the fact that there *is* hope; you *can* step outside of the box and not only survive, but flourish. I once felt nothing would ever change; I thought that I had no purpose in life. But there is a purpose for each and every one of us.

All three of my kids—especially Tamara—are so much happier now that we all have such a true and strong connection, now that I'm not giving them the "Momma gotta work" excuse.

Last year, I got a Mother's Day card from my youngest son that read, *Thank you, Mom, for teaching us to eat healthier now.* I'd been speaking to them about the importance of eating healthfully, and it was huge that I was making my own shifts and communicating them to my kids. They were able to listen, because they *had* someone to be an example for them and show them love, and to follow the new patterns I was creating.

What new patterns could you create when you step out of the box?

Latonya Collins is a mom of three who has found her life's passion in writing and in helping others to overcome life's obstacles by overcoming her own. She has a gift for helping those who are sick and tired of going in circles in life, who want to see their desires fulfilled, but don't know where to start. To learn more about breaking your cycle and stepping out of your box, visit www.LatonyaCollins.com.

Lauren Ellerbeck

ARE YOU LISTENING?

It was a beautiful sunny day when I graduated from Le Cordon Bleu culinary school in Austin, Texas. I was proud of my accomplishment and I worked hard to complete the program but, unlike my fellow graduates, I was not excited about my future. Coming out of the school after graduation, I realized, *I don't want to be a chef. I have to follow my heart. But what does that mean?*

I had a hunch that I wanted to become an entrepreneur and I was interested in real estate, but I had no idea where to start or whom to turn to for advice. For a long time after that I struggled, looking for answers. So I started attending business networking meetings once a month to search and to learn.

Because I was unsure about my career path, it was challenging to connect with people at the networking events. I kept hitting brick walls, which left me feeling frustrated and lonely. At the events members occasionally got up and gave a thirty second speech about themselves, and afterward I said, "Can someone be honest with me? How am I coming off when I'm standing up there? I need an honest opinion."

One of the members came up to me and said, "You should talk to Monty. He's in real estate, your field. He'd be happy to give you feedback."

In his forties, Monty had years of experience in real estate and he *was* happy to give me feedback; it was such a relief. He had all of the knowledge I had been searching for. He pointed out that I didn't have the support I needed to move toward the goals I wanted to achieve.

"I'm ready to learn, and I'll go to work," I said.

I was so happy when Monty replied, "You need a mentor. You don't have to do this alone. Let's work together."

Procrastination has always been a challenge for me. There are so many distractions—my phone goes, the dog needs to go out, something needs to be cleaned. When I procrastinate, the

I wanted to become an entrepreneur.

guilt piles up and I find myself avoiding even the simplest tasks. When Monty started coaching me on the philosophy of Gary Keller's book *The One Thing*, all of that changed.

Monty taught me about the power of doing one thing that is productive, that even the smallest progress can make the biggest difference. He asked me to practice daily accountability:

1. Did you get your one thing done today?
2. How does that make you feel?
3. What are you going to do differently tomorrow?
4. Now press the reset button and put "one thing" on your calendar.

It sounds simple, but it's been a huge help to me as I move forward toward my goals. At the end of the day, talking over my "one thing" progress with Monty helped me to understand the flow of feeling confident. When I completed an activity—my one thing—in line with my goals I felt amazing. When I didn't get it done that day, the old guilt came back. Soon, I was knocking out my one thing most days and those one things all added up to something I had been longing for, for a long time: the start of a real career.

Early on in my mentoring relationship with Monty he asked, "Do you want me to tell you what you want to hear, or what you need to hear?"

I used to be resistant to criticism. While still in culinary school I worked in a very high-end, high-stress kitchen and any time someone criticized me I would burst into tears and say, "I can't handle this!" Not all criticism is welcome, but the benefit of the mentor relationship is you've agreed to work with this person who has your best interests at heart.

I realized I didn't have to react the same way to Monty's feedback because I knew his intentions. It took me a while to work up to being able to handle constructive criticism from

---

**You need a mentor. You don't
have to do this alone.**

Monty, but now I see his feedback as positive. And I know now that paying attention to what I need to hear brings permanent change. I learn more from well-intentioned criticism than I would from hearing, "Good job making that phone call."

The other day Monty and I went into a meeting. Afterwards he said, "What you're wearing is not business casual. It's dressy, going-out casual." I was hurt at first; I thought I knew what business casual was. But I quickly reminded myself that Monty was acting as my mirror, showing me something I couldn't see myself, something I could do differently to help me get where I wanted to go.

The coolest thing about working with Monty is he boosts my confidence when he edifies me. It's as though he's my personal spokesman. After years of feeling frustrated and confused about what to do next, it feels amazing to have a mentor who has confidence in me. It makes me feel as though I could do anything!

Having a mentor is much like football. There are players on the field, coaches on the sidelines and spokespeople in the skybox. They all have different roles, but work together for one purpose—to create an outcome working as a team. In this analogy, the mentee is the football player and the mentor is the coach. The football player listens to the coach and takes some risks based on his guidance. The team might get tackled but they've got to get back up so the mentee can get a touchdown! The people in the skybox can see the bigger picture of the play-by-play, giving more feedback.

When I have been the football player, I am way too close to see any other way but what's right in front of me. Sometimes I need the skybox perspective; sometimes I need advice from my

Paying attention to what I need to
hear brings permanent change.

coaches. When someone helps me to win and go higher, it also helps them feel like a champion, celebrating the success they helped me to create!

Everyone wants to be on a winning team together. How fun is it to be successful when there's no one on the mountain top with you, nobody to share the win with or pat you on the back? True success is who I bring along with me. I was looking for a place to belong and fit in. I found it, and now I want to help those that feel the same way find a place to win in all aspects of life.

Facing the truth isn't easy. But if you look at the flip side of it, it's rare to have the opportunity to be mentored. It's rare to have a friend point out ways you could make improvements to get you closer to where you want to go. It's rare to have access to the wisdom of ordinary people achieving extraordinary things.

Be grateful for the mirrors in life.

The other authors in this book have a lot of accomplished a lot and I'm just getting started. But what I learned from my mentoring experience is helpful for anyone. I learned how to be coachable, to be willing and open, to accept the truth about myself and to really listen to what my mentor had to say. I try to set my ego and pride aside in favor of becoming the person I want to be, and in doing that I am making the most of my mentorship experience.

How do you make the most of getting information, inspiration and guidance? What are you going to do with it? Being coachable is being willing to listen, and learn, and correct and move forward. How are you going to get the most from your mentors? Your coaches? Your teachers? Seminars, workshops, classes? How are you going to get the most from this book?

Are you willing to be coached? Are you paying attention? Are you listening?

Lauren Ellerbeck is beginning her real estate career and business, Hope Investments Group, with Keller Williams. Her motivation and fulfillment comes from helping people and giving them hope—consulting with clients to help them create a plan to make their dream of home ownership a tangible reality and working with distressed sellers who want to prevent a short sale or foreclosure of the home. She is excited about working with her mentor and business partner, Monty Maulding, who was personally and voluntarily mentored by Gary Keller, founder of Keller Williams. Together they help others start their real estate businesses.

Lauren believes strongly in mentoring and empowering children and paying it forward for all of the life-changing mentoring she received. She has recently become a Big Sister with Big Brothers Big Sisters. She also partners with the William Walsh Foundation in support of Big Brothers Big Sisters. In her spare time she enjoys painting and jogging around the lake with her German Shepard/Lab mix, Rocky. To learn more about becoming a Big Brothers Big Sisters mentor or a mentee child, visit www.BBBS.org. To connect with Lauren visit www. HopeInvestmentsGroup.com.

Cheryl Desaritz

Walk Away

I stood at the second story window, so unhappy, contemplating: *Should I jump? Would that get me out of this marriage that torments me so much? After fifteen years, can I just end it all with one leap? Unfortunately, it's not that far to the ground. I'll probably just break a leg and, if I die, he will raise our son.*

How had I come to this—contemplating suicide because my life was so miserable? I had a great childhood, for the most part. I had two loving parents and two fun-loving siblings. Dad and I were introverts in a houseful of extroverts, so we had a hard time getting a word in edgewise. Money was an issue and I often heard, "We can't afford that; money doesn't grow on trees." I don't remember talking about college and a possible career—probably "we couldn't afford it." I was expected to marry and have a family.

I was the shy kid, feeling unhappy; thinking *I don't belong;* thinking *I'm not pretty enough, popular enough, thin enough.* Kids like to bully and pick on those more vulnerable. What was it about me that let others think it was okay to abuse me? It seemed I wore a sign on my back: "Cheryl will take anything you throw at her."

My tag line was: *Things don't bother me; I let things roll off my shoulders.* So I thought. Truth be told, I buried things, buried them deep down inside. All that garbage eventually, without my realizing it, built a wall around my inner being, my heart and soul.

When I was sixteen, my best friend introduced me to her cousin, who lived in Brooklyn. We lived out on Long Island. We became three best friends. I wanted my girlfriend from Brooklyn at my sweet sixteen party. The only way she could get there was if her older brother drove her. He was invited and the unexpected happened; we became an item.

What more could I ask for: great friends, a terrific party and now a new beau? Life was good. It started out to be a wonderful relationship. I believe we both were very happy and very much in love.

Not quite two years later, we married. I believed that when you got married, marriage was forever. No ifs, ands or buts—marriage was forever. My parents begged me not to get married. They said I was too young. I'm sure his parents felt the same way, even though he was a couple of years older.

Because we were the first of our friends to wed, our home was a gathering place for weekends. We had so much fun! We partied, we drank and we danced—*until* my husband got drunk and sick.

Whether we were home or we went out, he drank too much and then, without fail, he got sick. After a while it was old hat. Inevitably, just before we went out, he'd cause a fight. He tortured

I wanted this marriage and I would learn to make it work. However, I was the only one working on it.

me, not physically, verbally. When we went out to a restaurant, no matter where they seated us, he didn't like the table. He wanted a booth; he didn't want a booth. Anything to cause a scene. I think he lived to make my life miserable. It was like living with a two year old who threw a tantrum whenever he wanted something.

He'd say, "Drinking makes me feel better about myself; it brings me out of my shell." And to an extent, it did. Unfortunately, he had no limit to his drinking, none. He drank until he got sick. One night he drove home; I slept. I was awakened by honking horns.

He was driving on the wrong side of the highway. Thank goodness, he didn't cause an accident; no one was hurt. That was the last time I took a drink; I was now the designated driver.

At my brother-in-law's Bar Mitzvah, a dancing partner asked me if I was happy.

I replied, "Is anyone really ever totally happy?"

I should have known right then and there that something was not right. I knew I wasn't happy, yet I honestly believed there was no perfect marriage. I believed marriage was forever, it's an adjustment. *I can handle anything, right? I'm a grown woman; it's time I acted the part.* I wanted this marriage and I would learn to make it work. However, I was the only one working on it.

Feel it, deep within your heart, feel the pain. Bring it to the surface and let it out.

Every week I went to bingo with his mom and his sister, my best friend. I couldn't get out the door without him starting a fight with me, even though most of the time he came with us. I was not allowed to have a good time, with him or without him. My relationship with my sister also suffered. Every time we visited her and her family—I swear, every time—my spouse started a fight with me. Our friends stopped inviting us—his drinking was more than they could handle. My spouse was working very hard to isolate me from friends and family.

His rages were terrifying. He would break things, especially my favorite things, and scream insults and profanities like a lunatic. I don't think I knew I was being abused. I was in love and marriage was forever. I knew I could fix him: make him stop drinking; show him that when he drank he wasn't very nice to me. Make him aware that other people were excluding us from their lives. *Why doesn't he see that he's hurting me, the girl he fell in love with?*

Once I took my son to a family support group that helps family members understand and cope with their situations—to support each other and share their stories on how to deal with life as it is.

Some of the stories would make your hair stand up. I wanted to run, screaming. It was definitely not the type of encouragement or support I needed or wanted. I needed someone to tell me to get the hell out of there. Someone to coax me, cheer me on, tell me that I could do it and that I could make it alone (with my son).

I can't tell you how many times I would check my finances to see if I could live on my salary. I pondered this for years. My son and I on our own, without a man in my life—it was scary. Yet, staying in the marriage was more terrifying.

Then I overheard Mom ask her friend, "After all these years, how can you stay with him, with the way he treats you and talks to you?"

Her friend answered, "I had no place to go and now I'm seventy years old. Where would I go? It's too late."

At that very moment, I knew one thing: *I don't want to be seventy and still miserable.* It was time to walk away.

If someone in your life is making you unhappy—maybe a spouse, or a friend, or a relative, or a boss, or a co-worker—my journey in walking away can help you take your own steps. If the abuse is physical, it's very important that you get help in planning your exit, because leaving can be dangerous for you.

You have to really search inside yourself. Ask yourself, "Is this the way I want to live my life?" Are you going to let him control you and treat you like garbage? When is your time to stand up tall and say, "*No more*"?

Emotional soul-searching takes work. You need to be in a quiet place—no distractions, none. First, you need to face the truth. Go as far back as you can and remember. Dig deep, deeper than you have ever done before. Feel it, deep within your heart, feel the pain. Bring it to the surface and let it out.

Not until we recondition our own minds can we recover, rebuild and redesign our own lives. Write down those feelings, the anger, sorrow and hatred. Use a different sheet of paper for each person who hurt you. Say from the bottom of your heart, "Thank you for sharing your thoughts. I forgive you. I will no longer carry this with me. I forgive you. Your words no longer have any effect on me." Now tear it up, shred it, trash it or take it outside and burn it. Let it go and say, "Thank you, thank you, thank you." Most of all, forgive yourself for holding on to this for so long.

After years of working at this marriage, really trying to change him, I couldn't take it anymore. I didn't want him anymore. It was a Saturday morning. My son was playing in his bedroom; my spouse and I were having coffee at the dining room table. After months in and out of counseling, contemplating being in and out of the marriage, we looked at each other and we both knew it wasn't going to work. It was over. He went apartment hunting and I went to my parents. I cried. I told them I couldn't do it anymore—work on a

---

*We were all meant to live a life
of joy and abundance.*

---

marriage that was painful and now loveless. I needed and wanted more out of life. They understood and took me in their arms to comfort me. The comfort of loving arms, how I had missed that!

I was so frightened, afraid of the unknown, of what tomorrow would bring. I knew with the love and support of my parents I could walk away and start a new life for me and my son. A life of hope and joy, with laughter and fun times. A life we both deserved.

You've taken the first step toward finding what you really want in life, walking away from the hurt and into a life filled with joy. That is true success—waking up every morning greeting each beautiful day with happiness and joy, doing what your heart tells you is your destiny. We were all meant to live a life of joy and abundance; it's our birthright.

Life isn't easy; yet, it should be your choice if you want to stay in a relationship or go. If you can't do it alone, there are places— shelters, agencies—you can turn to. No one can do this for you. We can only help you through it. We all have the strength to walk away. It took me eight years to get out of that marriage, eight long, hard, unhappy years. Just take it one step at a time.

Cheryl Desaritz has married again and is the mom and stepmom of three children. She has seven grandchildren. She has redefined herself and is now taking courses to become a transformational coach. She plans to be a speaker and is writing the forthcoming book: Abuse is Unacceptable: The Strength to Walk Away. *Connect with Cheryl at www.SuccessCoachForLife.com.*

Christene Cronin

LOVING THE PROCESS
OF SUCCESS

Isn't it wonderful to achieve success? Or perhaps you are on your way to achieving it—doesn't it fill you with joy every day? Maybe not. You got that promotion, but you're working twelve-hour days seven days a week. You're your own boss, but every one of your clients is monopolizing your time. You thought you had enough cash reserve to strike out on your own, but your spouse is getting testy about finding the money to pay the bills. And your kids are upset because you spent the family vacation working on your laptop.

You reached a big milestone: your first client; the project that will get you promoted; your thousandth sale or your first million dollars. But instead of celebrating, you immediately set another goal and put your nose back to the grindstone.

The path to success is stressful and your body is sending you warning signals. Maybe a voice in your head tells you to slow down. Maybe your stomach is tight or your eye twitches on a regular basis. Maybe you just can't say "no" and you have strong feelings of guilt. Maybe you constantly bite your lip. These are all triggers, alerting you that your stress level is damaging. For me, it was my jaw. I was grinding my teeth so hard at night and during the day that I cracked teeth. But, like you, I'm energetic, ambitious and driven. I can handle anything, so I ignored the trigger.

After about ten years in the information technology (IT) arena, I achieved my goal to become an IT leader for a software development company. I was so excited! I received a large increase in pay, my own parking spot, a team of professionals to lead and thirty small business clients with whom to build relationships. It was a dream come true.

However, as I discovered, my new department had major issues. Three leaders before me had quickly come and gone. I had employees who were angry, or incapable, or who wanted to move out of the department, or who had a chip on their shoulder. One client was going to picket the company if we didn't fix all the bugs in our software. Then after about three months into the company, my director handed me the support department to manage as well. One of the women there felt she should have my job. But all that was okay, because I love to help people and my analytical mind loves to solve problems. I had succeeded in reaching my goal.

My husband at the time and his partner were just starting their own software company. So now two of us were experiencing new major responsibilities in our careers. Neither of us expressed our emotions in a healthy way. We would bury issues or problems that came up because we just wanted to feel happy.

I worked long hours, all night sometimes, and worked weekends, so I had lost closeness with family and a few friends. My in-laws lived with us, which I thought was fine as we did have a good relationship, but I had lost my privacy. I had nowhere to go to relax and unwind.

The pressure was building at home, in my personal life and at work. I felt angry all the time; I had very little patience; I would be short and abrupt with people and was not my usual happy, outgoing self. I would grind my teeth so hard at night that I would wake up with a sore jaw. Eventually I cracked the bottom row of my teeth on the right side.

And then it happened. I was driving home from work one day when my jaw locked open. I could not close it at all. I had been feeling tense all over, gripping the steering wheel with all my might. By the time I got home, I felt drained and scared. I knew I needed help, but didn't know where to get it. The next two days I called in sick at work and spent my time at a nearby lake, where I watched the water and the people enjoying it, gradually letting go of the tension and getting a grasp of my situation.

I was raised to look after myself and not to ask for help, as that was a sign of weakness (limiting belief). If I couldn't afford something, then I didn't deserve it (limiting belief). If we children did something wrong, we got the silent treatment from the whole family—no discussions about what happened, or how to overcome

I had succeeded in reaching my goal.

the problem, just the silent treatment. So as time went on, if something was wrong in my personal relationships, I believed it was best to just keep quiet.

In the business world however, I was able to deal with the facts and go to the source of the problem and manage it effectively. I was quite capable of acting on and resolving issues and conflicts with ease. Yet in my personal life, I worried about hurting other's feelings, even at the expense of my own.

I did not give myself recognition for major accomplishments I made, like meeting unrealistic deadlines, bringing in new business or the successful implementation of new technology. And I definitely did not recognize all the many small accomplishments along the way.

I did not stop to realize that each step forward I took, each new piece of knowledge I gained, each client whose trust I captured with ease or employee I guided in their career, was a stepping stone or milestone to reaching that goal of being successful, a process that happens to all of us.

During this time, I came across a booked called *The Essence of Happiness* by the Dalai Lama and Dr. Howard Cutler, psychologist. I immediately turned to the chapter on anger. *What do you mean? Anger is a feeling; you can't stop it.* The book describes the negative states of mind that destroy our happiness and how we can overcome them. *I can change my own feelings.* I now knew I had to have the difficult conversations with the people who were close to me in my personal life about my need for privacy. And that started me on my path to releasing the anger, anxiety and frustration I was feeling constantly. However, it took many more books over many more years and another burnout to really understand how to look after myself emotionally.

And when the Institute of Social and Emotional Intelligence came into my life it was a God-send. I learned more about self-awareness, one of the most fundamental and essential of all the twenty-six competences of social and emotional intelligence. I

I can change my own feelings.

---

learned how to use it to further assist myself as well as my clients to be aware of the emotions we feel in the moment and then learn to manage those feelings effectively. I know now that the tension in my jaw is a trigger, my body's way of warning me that I have too much stress in my life.

I internally search out the problem and manage it; I don't wait until stress damages my body. I no longer deceive myself into thinking things are okay when they are not or give myself an excuse to avoid a personal issue or situation. I can speak up and discuss my feelings openly with anyone who oversteps my boundaries. I can identify the symptoms and signs of stress and then take action to manage it and I feel so much better for that. I am being true to who I am, not trying to be like someone else. Knowledge of who we are and what we value and believe is power. And the real power is found by living our lives based on our values and beliefs, without fear of any kind.

Before we start a business, or even now while we are in the throes of our business, if we could look at all the aspects of what it takes to be "successful," if we could break it down into the skills required emotionally as well as intellectually, we could save ourselves from an awful lot of unhappiness, fear and excessive stress. We could effectively be prepared and better able to handle any adversity.

My theory is, success is a process and, unless you decide to end this quest, project or goal, it will continue to be an ongoing process. You will make many mistakes; you'll have many peaks and valleys and question your reason for doing what you are doing. Just know that you are not alone! It happens to everyone!

With my current career as an emotional intelligence coach, consultant and public speaker, I am handling each obstacle I overcome with greater resiliency and acknowledging that I did so. I am giving myself permission to make mistakes and learn from them. I even ask for help when I need it.

I enjoy each new accomplishment I make and give myself credit where it is due, on a regular basis. If we can do this for an employee, we can certainly do it for ourselves. It makes the process much more enjoyable. I know that there will always be some difficulties in my life from time to time, but I also know that if I keep moving forward with focus on my goals, they soon will pass.

Not long ago, I had a coach who was more aggressive than assertive and found fault rather than made suggestions. I woke one

---

Be kind to yourself.

---

morning with a sore jaw. I'd been grinding my teeth all night. I was busy and just ignored it. But when I woke the next morning with the same soreness, I responded to my trigger. It didn't take long to identify the source of my stress. I ended the coaching relationship immediately. When my jaw gets tight because of something unavoidable like a tight deadline, I reassess the situation and I am kind to myself by finding a way to truly relax, even if it's just enjoying a cup of tea while I think things through.

So with a clear picture of my goals, I am armed with an abundance of patience, realizing that it is going to take time to get where I am going. I recognize each new growth spurt, as I like to call it, whether it is a major milestone or a minor one, and focus on the positives. I continue to educate myself and this time around I am consciously enjoying the ongoing process of my new success.

I think you've got to be driven and have passion to sustain a business. You can pull all-nighters and work weekends and love it. But it's vital that you also be self-aware; heed what your body is telling you. When you feel a trigger, use your resilience to dig out of the stress. Be kind to yourself; exercise and take care of your health. Build your self-confidence. Even the most successful people have dips in their confidence; the ones who continue on their road to success are the ones who know how to reignite themselves.

Find your joy; what makes you laugh out loud on a regular basis? Strive with all your might to be true to yourself and live your values and then ask for help to get there!

Christene Cronin worked for over twenty years in the information technology (IT) world as a software developer/analyst, technical consultant, IT leader and project manager. She was responsible for gaining clients' trust and confidence, providing the best solution for their business needs and helping them recognize the value and benefits of the technology. In addition, she helped her team develop business knowledge and acumen, professionalism and communication skills.

In 2001, Christene ventured into direct sales, tapping into her background of selling IT services and effectively managing and building relationships. In 2009, she pursued certification first as a coach and then in emotional intelligence, where she discovered her talent for empowering people to achieve their goals. Discovering You was born. She realized that, though her clients sought her out for help with business issues, most of them had more personal self-doubt and conflict issues. The challenges experienced by Christene and her clients fueled her passion and drive to help entrepreneurs and business professionals avoid burn out and find their joy.

Christene is a speaker and consultant and offers one-to-one coaching and corporate workshops. Her community involvement includes mentoring immigrant women who hope to start a business. Connect with Christene at www.DiscoveringYou.ca.

Steven H. Poulos, DDS

JUST KEEP DOING

We all have preconceived notions about what we can do and what we are willing to do. But life has a tendency to set up roadblocks, and that's when you just have to keep doing. Maybe it's as simple as getting your hands dirty, hauling your own trash to the dump. Maybe you need to learn a new skill so you can do your own bookkeeping. And sometimes it's both getting your hands dirty and learning a new skill, as when Steven the dentist learned to become Steven the carpenter, hanging the cabinets in my new dental office.

My family and I loved Scottsdale, Arizona. The climate was delightful and the schools were excellent; the community offered many opportunities for recreation and entertainment. And we could live with my wife's cousins while we looked for a house.

But setting up a dental practice on a shoestring is daunting. I found a good location in a shopping center, but it had been a retail shop. The carpet was worn; the décor was bland and uninviting. And of course, it had no examination rooms with plumbing and vacuum systems, X-ray machines or any of the other equipment a dental office needs.

Ideally, I would hire a specialist contractor and just walk into my brand new office after six carefree months, the space converted as though by a magic wand. A magic wand and a ton of money.

I couldn't afford to hire a specialist to convert the space. But I kept doing. I hired a general contractor on a part-time basis and planned to do some of the work myself. According to the plan, the conversion would take about six months and I would be seeing my first patients in January. In October, the contractor quit. The sinks still weren't in, the walls were still ugly and the old cabinets still hung there.

It's unnerving when a plan fails, but you have to keep on doing. I was definitely unnerved, but I was determined to make another plan and work at it. I had a commitment to my wife and children and nothing would stop me from opening my practice. No matter what obstacles came up, I was still going to finish that office.

I kept doing. I'd never hung cabinets before, but I learned. When I took the old cabinets down, I took note of how the screws fit into the wall. I bought a saw and a level at Home Depot and, with help from my nephew, learned how to hang cabinets. The woman who sold me the countertops took the necessary measurements and guided us in installing them. Steven the dentist was proud of the work Steven the carpenter had accomplished.

Next, my wife and I tackled the office décor. My cousin's wife helped us wallpaper the front office and paint the other walls in

---

It's unnerving when a plan fails, but you have to keep on doing.

---

cheerful colors. We found good art for the waiting areas, as well as some of those cute posters you see in dental offices.

I still didn't have sinks in the examination rooms—those sinks next to the chairs, the ones that you lean over when the dentist says, "Rinse and spit." But often when you just keep doing, luck favors you and a way past the roadblock appears, almost as if by magic. Bill Barrio, a dental supplier, found vacuum-operated dental sinks, solving the plumbing problem. I ordered eight of them. Bill directed me to Roger, who installed the vacuum lines and put in the water and drain pipes.

The vacuum lines were a godsend, but they looked ugly. I decided to surround them with a soffit, a sort of arched overhang. I'd hung the cabinets; I should be able to make a soffit. As I was struggling with the forty-five degree angles of the corners, Dr. Michael Bubeck, whose office was down the hall and who was quite a carpenter, offered the loan of a miter saw. I'd never heard of a miter saw, but it helped me make lovely corners.

I was well on my way to having a professional office; now I needed to let my prospective patients know about my practice. Way back then, dentists only advertised in the telephone book's yellow pages. Unfortunately, we had moved to Scottsdale just after the publication deadline for the phone book. We wouldn't be

---

Nothing builds confidence like overcoming
a seemingly insurmountable obstacle.

---

mentioned, let alone have an ad, for another eleven months. Again, I kept on doing. My wife and I brainstormed about advertising. We had business cards printed and took them to the other shops in the mall, asking the shop owners to help spread the word about my dental practice—and that bore fruit, but not right away. We needed another advertising vehicle, so we kept doing.

In December, we offered a discount coupon in a Val-Pack, which was given free to mall customers. In January, the answering machine tape was full, all month long. But the office wasn't quite ready. Another roadblock.

We called those prospective patients back, saying, "We're fully booked for January. Would you like to make an appointment for February?"

At last, the office was ready. How many seemingly insurmountable obstacles I had overcome! How many times I was at the point of tears, thinking, *Oh gosh, I can't pull this off!* But I had kept doing, no matter what. I felt well-earned pride as I strode into the warm, welcoming waiting area and inspected the examination rooms—one last time—to make sure everything was ready. Not only had I created an office for my practice, I had also become more self-confident and savvier about business.

Nothing builds confidence like overcoming a seemingly insurmountable obstacle. Dental schools can sap students' self-confidence. Professors are often like drill sergeants in boot camp. It's unnerving enough to approach a patient's mouth with sharp

*You can get past any roadblock
if you keep doing.*

instruments and a high-speed drill without having your professor pointing out every error or hesitation in the most uncomplimentary terms. Over time, the constant criticism might make students better dentists, but it also does deep damage to their self-confidence.

Furthermore, dental schools don't offer a single course in the business aspects of maintaining a practice. Dentists graduate without knowing how to compose an effective advertisement, or build referrals or even read an accountant's balance sheet. Being my own contractor, working within a limited budged and finding unconventional ways to advertise my practice had taught me a lot about business—lessons I would apply as I built my practice.

In a few months, my practice was profitable. In about five years, I moved to a larger space. But all the things I had learned when converting a retail store to a dental office stayed with me. As I looked at my professional colleagues, I saw how difficult it could be to overcome a lack of self-confidence and a lack of business expertise. Young dentists have larger debts now than they did thirty years ago. They face more competition and find fewer places in which to set up practices. They need help and guidance in getting established. I had lessons to share with them.

So I founded the Professional Success Institute to help dentists and other professionals achieve success in work and in personal life. For non-dentists, I co-founded the SEO Maximum Performance Group. One of the lessons I teach—and it applies to everyone—is, when Plan A fails, don't waste time lamenting or whining about it.

Go on to Plan B. You can have the greatest strategy in the world, but sometimes obstacles will come up that prevent you from executing it. When that happens, just keep doing.

The main thing is to have the moxie or self-determination to finish, no matter what. Maybe you don't know how to keep accurate accounts. Is there an adult education course, or online instruction in bookkeeping you can take? Can you pay an accountant to show you how? If you can't afford a carpenter to install the shelves you need, you can learn to do it yourself. (Measure twice, cut once.) Maybe your business needs better marketing and public relations. Your local library has or can order many good resource books that will get you started and encourage you to try various approaches, approaches your competition hasn't even considered.

You can get past any roadblock if you keep doing. When one thing doesn't work, don't waste time moping or spend your mental energy being discouraged. Just pull up your socks and do something.

Life and business require the proper mindset, development of a proper strategy and massive action. If at first you fail, make a new plan and work that plan until you succeed. Just keep doing!

Steven H. Poulos, DDS, has seen more than thirty thousand patients, completed more than three hundred thousand procedures and generated more than thirty million dollars in revenue. Dr. Poulos earned his Doctor of Dental Surgery degree at Creighton University in 1979. He specializes in helping anxious patients overcome dental fears, reconstructions of complex dental problems, cosmetic makeovers, emergency care, implant dentistry, children's dentistry and advanced periodontic care. He is a Fellow of the Academy of General Dentistry and a member of the American Dental Association, the Arizona State Dental Association, the Central Arizona Dental Society and the American Academy of Cosmetic Dentistry. He practices at North Scottsdale Family and Cosmetic Dentistry in Scottsdale, Arizona.

Dr. Poulos founded the Professional Success Institute to help dentists win in their practice. Pioneering the "Bread and Butter and Caviar" style of practice, his seminars, audio and videotape programs and his in-office consulting services have helped many dentists develop a more profitable and enjoyable practice. His focus is on whole-person success. Winning dentists balance health, family, relationships, spiritual and community components so they can optimize their practices, making them win-win-win for patients, staff and doctors. To bring this strategy to non-dentists, he co-founded SEO Maximum Performance Group, a program designed to help any business, author or movie producer market their product or services either online or in a brick-and-click mode.

Dr. Poulos has written two books: Secret Weapons for Painless Dentistry *and* Secret Weapons for Success. *He is available for speaking engagements, seminars or private consulting. Connect with Dr. Poulos at www.ProfessionalSuccessInstitute.com.*

Dr. Eric Wong

SMALL STEPS TO BIG CHANGES

As Mrs. X left the examination room, the door closing softly behind her, I could hear again the despair in her voice. "Dr. Wong, the medicine you've given me for my emphysema is keeping me alive, but I'm so short of breath I can't leave my house. Just washing my few dishes wears me out and I have to sit down. I miss people! I miss my friends at my craft circle; I miss going to church. I couldn't even go to my grandson's basketball games."

There must be something I can do to help Mrs. X improve her quality of life, I thought. Mrs. X was a widow in her late sixties. She had been active in her family, church and community until emphysema restricted her activities. Emphysema reduces the elasticity of a patient's lungs so that they cannot exhale fully. Its symptoms begin with shortness of breath and progress until, as for Mrs. X, every breath is a struggle. As a pulmonologist, an expert in lung diseases, I could keep her breathing, but living fully is more than just breathing.

Most of my patients have chronic conditions; I see them often and come to know them well, so being unable to further help Mrs. X and patients like her grieved me.

And then I remembered: Mrs. X had stopped smoking, but she still breathed in the same pattern as a smoker does. She took a long, deep breath in and then exhaled as quickly as possible. I knew reversing that pattern, taking quick breaths in and exhaling slowly, was helpful for emphysema patients. Could Mrs. X learn a new habit? And if she did, would it make a difference in her life?

On her next visit, I showed her the better breathing pattern and explained why it could help her. We practiced together. She promised to keep practicing until the new pattern was natural.

When she returned some weeks later, she was not the dejected Mrs. X that I was used to seeing.

"Dr. Wong," she said, "I can wash dishes, sweep the floor, wipe down the counters and I still don't have to sit down. I even went to church last Sunday."

One small step, one changed habit—and her life was so much better!

Over the next months, my team and I helped Mrs. X make other small changes, such as changing the position in which she slept and doing muscle-strengthening exercises with small weights. I encouraged her to walk daily, either inside or outside. By the end of the year, she was meeting her craft circle and attending family events—she had her life back. What's more, she had built reserves of strength she could call on when she was stressed or had an illness.

I could keep her breathing, but living
fully is more than just breathing.

Small steps bring huge changes—not just for pulmonary disease patients, but for everyone. When I was a tutor during my university years, I helped other students make small steps that helped them succeed. I remember one woman who was having trouble with math.

Her learning style was out of sync with both the textbook and the teacher. When I was able to use real-world examples, she learned quickly and was able to pass the course with a good grade.

Similarly, when I learn a new procedure in pulmonology, I break it down into the smallest steps and then examine each one. I ask myself: *How can this small step be improved?* Often, improving one tiny step has a big impact on the whole procedure.

What changes do you want to make in your life? Maybe you want to be more physically fit. Losing weight and exercising is a major change and can be daunting. But can you add one serving of vegetables and one serving of fruit every day? After that becomes a habit, maybe you can substitute whole grain bread for white bread. Can you park a block from your destination to add some walking to your day?

As each small step becomes a habit and you notice the impact it has on your well-being, you'll find it easier and easier to take the next small step.

Improving one tiny step has a big impact on the whole procedure.

I've noticed two things that keep people from taking small steps toward big changes. First is a lack of confidence in their ability to learn anything new. So often children run into teachers who don't understand and accommodate their individual learning styles. Then the children, and later the adults, have no confidence that they can learn, they can exchange habits for better ones. The key is to ignore the negative, such as "I just am not an organized person," and make one small step. Declutter one drawer—with piles to toss, to move somewhere else and to put back. One drawer is not a major commitment—it's just a small step.

Second is a difficulty in identifying the small steps to take. If you want to become a more successful entrepreneur, for instance, you may have trouble deciding just where to start. A mentor can be very helpful in pointing out what is holding you back. Perhaps you need more accounting skills and should take a class. Maybe you need help with public speaking and should join a group that will encourage and educate you.

Look at what small steps you can take now to start changing your life for the better. And then begin to walk toward your personal success. Remember that changing habits takes practice. But the first step makes the second step easier as you see and feel the rewards for your efforts and gain confidence in your own ability to make changes. Just as Mrs. X and my other patients find that small changes bring big rewards, you will soon find yourself successful in your own life.

Dr. Eric Wong is a pulmonologist and an Associate Professor at the University of Alberta. He completed his medical training at University of Alberta and further training at McMaster University. He works with people with lung diseases in his clinical practice. Dr. Wong was the medical director for the Respiratory Outreach Program, a program working with people with advanced lung disease in the community. The insights gained in this chapter came from his own clinical practice and his work with the Respiratory Outreach Program.

MILLIONAIRE MIND COURSE CERTIFICATE

To reward you for taking the first step towards greater success by purchasing *The Spirit of Success,* Adam Markel and Peak Potentials is offering you and one guest an exclusive scholarship to attend the LIVE Millionaire Mind Intensive 3-day Seminar. At this world famous program, you can transform your Money Blueprint right there on site and change your financial life forever!

To register, visit www.millionairemindintensive.com and select the date and location of your choice.

Use Special Code AMAGIFT when you register.

PEAK POTENTIALS™

* This offer is open to all purchasers of *The Spirit of Success.* Limit one scholarship per copy of *The Spirit of Success.* Scholarship may only be applied to the Millionaire Mind Intensive 3-day Seminar and seminar registration is subject to availability and/or changes to program schedule. Additional fees and tuitions may apply at the time of registration. Registrants are responsible for travel, food and accommodation if required and are under no additional financial obligation whatsoever to Peak Potentials or Adam Markel. Peak Potentials reserves the right to refuse admission, and to remove from the premises anyone it believes is disrupting the seminar.

Free Gift from Bill Walsh

This invaluable Complete Business Package has everything you need to start, grow and possibly even double your business in the next 90 days.

Bill Walsh has helped business owners and entrepreneurs in more than thirty countries over the past two decades profit wildly with "inside-out" business consulting and proven marketing strategies. When you get this practical, step-by-step training system you will be introduced to specifically what it takes to create massive success in life and business! It is your turn for more time, money, wealth and happiness! **You will love the eMVP SUCCESSPACK!!!**

$497.00 Retail Value

Your Complimentary Digital Success Pack
www.eMVPsuccesspack.com code:7777

Join our Marketing Team Today
www.iPowerteam.biz